BECOMING
AN ANGLICAN

BECOMING AN ANGLICAN

— an Adult Confirmation Study Course

by

EDWARD H. PATEY

Dean Emeritus of Liverpool

MOWBRAY

Copyright © Edward H. Patey 1985

ISBN 0 264 67019 1

First published 1985 by Mowbray, Villiers House,
41–47 Strand, London, WC2N 5JE, a Cassell Company
Reprinted 1986, 1990, 1993

Typeset by Oxford Computer Typesetting
Printed in England by Clays Ltd, St Ives plc

British Library Cataloguing in Publication Data

Patey, Edward H.
  Becoming an Anglican. — (Popular Christian
  paperback series)
  1. Christian life — Anglican authors
  2. Confirmation — Anglican Communion
  I. Title   II. Series
  248.4'83   BV815

        ISBN 0-264-67019-1

FOREWORD

Edward Patey was a very special colleague in Liverpool. He was interested in every part of the life of the city, insisting that the Church is there not just for its own sake, but to serve real people in a real world. He gave a great lead to the growing ecumenical partnership between the Churches in Liverpool. At the same time he knew that each of us needs to be a loyal member of his own Church, which becomes like a springboard to launch us to serve God in the world with fresh love and hope.

Becoming an Anglican is always understandable; it doesn't pretend there are easy answers when there are not. That's where Edward Patey is a trustworthy guide. Soon after I became Bishop of Liverpool I was at a party for our own family. Two relatives from different sides of the family met for the first time. Both said that Edward Patey's writings had played a major part in bringing them back to faith. They told me that he didn't offer easy, complete packages of belief, which ignored the deep problems of life. They enjoyed reading his books, because they knew they were in the company of a human, thoughtful and believing Christian. They found he was good at asking questions which sparked off their own thoughts.

This book will provide an excellent study guide to adults who are preparing for Confirmation. I hope that many more, who are finding their way back into church life, or feel they need a refresher course, will use it. It fits very well with group study. It doesn't pretend that the Church is perfect; it calls us to follow Christ in a Christian company where honest thinking, beautiful worship, sensitivity to the needy and wholehearted service in the community make up the pattern we long for.

+ DAVID LIVERPOOL

Acknowledgements

Quotations from the New English Bible © 1970 by permission of Oxford and Cambridge University Presses.

Extracts from The Alternative Service Book 1980 are reproduced by permission of the Central Board of Finance of the Church of England.

To Bishop Michael Ramsey for allowing me to quote from *Be Still and Know* (Fount).

To Macmillan for a quotation from William Temple's *Readings in St John's Gospel*.

To Canon Frank Colquhoun for his willingness to allow me to include four prayers from his *Contemporary Parish Prayers* (Hodder & Stoughton).

E.H.P.

CONTENTS

1. INITIATION

Invitation to pilgrimage

You have made one of the greatest decisions of your life. Freely you have made up your mind to declare in public your faith in Jesus Christ and to commit yourself to him as a member of that world-wide family which is the Anglican Communion. This is the beginning of a long journey. You can only dimly understand what that decision may mean for you during the rest of your life. There are many things you do not yet understand, many questions yet to be asked and answered. You know that this is only the start of your pilgrimage of which the final destination remains hidden. But this is a common experience in many parts of life. A student leaves school to begin a course at university or college, unaware what kind of person will emerge from the process in three or four years' time. A person begins a new job not knowing where it will lead him. A young couple make their solemn vows in front of the altar with little understanding of what the experience of marriage and family life will bring them. When after great thought and preparation you finally decide to throw in your lot with Christ and his Church, the adventure which lies ahead may play as significant a part in your life story as home, marriage or job. These things may themselves be profoundly influenced by the decision you make to take Christian faith and membership seriously. It is hoped that this book will help you to follow through your decision to be confirmed, and to look forward to your life as a Christian with hope and expectation.

The following chapters are written to help you towards a fuller understanding of the faith you will profess, of the worship and prayers you will offer, and the practical service to the world you are bound to give. They will examine what it means to belong to a local congregation, to the Anglican Communion and to the world-wide Church of Jesus Christ. They will explore the style of life expected to be seen in a Christian as he fulfils his responsibility to his church, his family, his neighbourhood and himself. The closing pages will ask what should be your expectation as you come to the bishop to be confirmed, how you should prepare yourself for this great moment of commitment, and what it should mean to you when the bishop prays that you will daily increase in the Holy Spirit more and more.

These pages offer a do-it-yourself kit for those wishing to pledge themselves to Christian commitment. Like all DIY manuals it demands hard work from those who study it. Suggestions for prayer and Bible study need to be followed seriously. Questions for discussion must be carefully considered either privately or (better still) in a group with other adults following the same path. A limited number of inexpensive books are recommended and it would be a sensible addition to this preparation course to make time to read some of them. Regular attendance at your local church is obviously an essential requirement for those preparing for adult baptism and confirmation, and the material in this study should help you to share in the worship and teaching of your church with more understanding, and perhaps more critically as well. This book will not provide you with all the answers you want. Some of the profoundest questions which life raises will not be answered, or only partially, this side of the grave. Throughout your life as a Christian you will experience moments of doubt as well as of assurance. When one set of questions has been answered, new ones will take their place to bewilder you. That is part of the Christian adventure. This is also the reason why, even more important than your own reading and thinking, you need to seek help from other people who may be a little further ahead of you on the Christian pilgrimage. You should look for encouragement and enlightenment, not only from clergy (that is part of their job), but from other lay people whose experience of Christian faith and life may be invaluable to you.

Joining

The Christian religion is not simply a set of ideas about God and the world which a large number of people happen to share. Essential to Christianity is the concept of membership. The consequence of belief in God as revealed in the Bible, and especially in the life and teaching of Jesus Christ is the necessity of belonging. As we shall see later, there can be no Christianity without the Church. Belonging is a necessary part of believing.

The second chapter of the Acts of the Apostles gives a marvellous picture of the very first days of the Christian Church. After the experience of the descent of the Holy Spirit on the disciples assembled in the upper room on the feast of Pentecost (verses 2-14), Peter preaches the first Christian sermon (verses 14-36). Its impact is so great that some three thousand people make an act of repentence, are promised the gift of the Spirit for themselves, and are baptized (verses 37-41). Immediately we see the Church springing into action. We are told that these new converts met constantly for instruction, for fellowship, for Communion and for prayer. And we are given a lively account of their new-found life-style.

'All whose faith had drawn them together held everything in common: they would sell their property and possessions and make a general distribution as the need of each required. With one mind they kept up their daily attendance at the temple, and, breaking bread in private houses, shared their meals with unaffected joy, as they praised God and enjoyed the favour of the whole people. And day by day the Lord added to their number those whom he was saving.'

Here we see the pattern of initiation into the Christian family which has, in various forms, been the practice of the Church ever since. The Gospel is preached. The hearers repent. They are promised the gift of the Spirit, and this is sealed in Baptism. Then they become part of a dynamic fellowship of Christian believers. Today all this has become formalized in the rites of Baptism and Confirmation. What is the relationship between the ceremonies as practised in the Anglican Church today, and those lively events described so vividly in the Acts of the Apostles?

Conversion

In the Bible accounts of life in the early days of the Church, it is clear that some kind of conversion was required before Baptism could be administered and the promise of the Spirit fulfilled. Does this correspond with your own experience and with what seems to be the present practice of your Church?

In The Alternative Service Book 1980 of the Church of England, the bishop says to the candidates who have come for Confirmation:

> 'Those of you who come to be confirmed must with your own mouth and from your own heart declare your allegiance to Christ and your rejection of all that is evil.'

This is followed by the three questions which repeat those already asked in the service of Baptism.

Do you turn to Christ?

Answer: I turn to Christ.

Do you repent of your sins?

Answer: I repent of my sins.

Do you renounce evil?

Answer: I renounce evil.

Nothing could be simpler or more direct than those simple questions and answers. This is the language of conversion. They speak of turning away from one mode of living and turning towards a quite different one. It is the assumption of the Anglican Church that those adults who come forward for Baptism and Confirmation have already been converted. But is this always to be taken for granted?

There are some people who in adolescence or in later life are so profoundly influenced by an evangelistic campaign (such as Billy Graham's 'Mission England' crusade in 1984), or by contact with a lively charismatic congregation or individual or in some other way, that they experience a personal crisis which compels them to change from a way of life in which religious faith and practice previously played no part, or from a nominal church membership which was largely an empty formality or social habit, to a deep conviction of Christ's personal call to them to repent of past life and to commit themselves to him for the rest of their days. Such people speak with utter conviction of the experience as having been 'born again', and can sometimes describe the exact time and place on which they surrendered themselves to the Lord. Such 'born again' Christians have a great contribution to bring to the life of the whole Church.

But it is not obligatory for all who claim to be Christians to have experienced this kind of dramatic conversion. The great majority of the most devoted and loyal church members have not had this experience, and could not give the date and place when they became Christians. For the majority the way to discipleship is through a gradual process, rather like the growing awareness that a child gains of his parents as he moves from infancy through childhood to adult life. Children may have a genuine experience of a loving relationship with Jesus Christ as they have with their father and mother. Yet the experience in early years is elementary and imitative. With growing up, the child's religious experience and understanding must become first hand and adult. This gradual process is no less a genuine experience of conversion than the more dramatic experience of being 'born again'. It may even indicate a deeper emotional maturity and roots which prove to be more durable.

Yet however it is achieved a genuine point of personal decision has to be reached. There must come a time when it can be said: 'I am a Christian because I have turned to Christ.' A second-hand religion passed on from the older generation must become a first-hand commitment. But this does not necessitate a particular moment when it can be claimed that, 'I have arrived', for even the most dramatic sudden conversion can generally be shown in analysis to have been part of a gradual process. At the height of his powers as a missionary theologian, Paul was honest enought to write to the Philippians, 'I have not yet reached perfection, but I press on, hoping to take hold of that for which Christ took hold of me. My friends, I do not reckon to have got hold of it yet. All I can say is this: forgetting what is behind me and reaching out for that which lies ahead, I press towards the goal.'[1] Conversion is an on-going process involving the whole of a person throughout the whole of his life. The adult who comes forward for Baptism and Confirmation has reached an important milestone. But it is only the start of the journey.

Baptism

Every society admits new members by some significant action, ranging from the signing of a membership form accompanied by the appropriate subscription, to the more elaborate rituals of the Boy Scouts or the Freemasons. These ceremonies are designed to impress upon the new member the seriousness of his decision and the significance of the institution he is about to join. From the earliest days of the Christian Church, the new convert has been admitted into membership by the initiation acts of Baptism and the laying on of hands following a declaration of penitence and an affirmation of belief. After Baptism and the laying on of hands the new Christian was admitted into the table fellowship of the Eucharist. This ancient tradition has been maintained by most parts of the Church, including those in the Anglican Communion, by Baptism (either in infancy or as an adult) and Confirmation.

In New Testament times candidates for Baptism were adults. This has continued to be so wherever mission churches have been breaking fresh ground in territories where the Gospel has not been heard before. Originally Baptism was a most solemn act in which the candidate was required to go down into the river and be immersed three times as a sign of initiation into the faith of the threefold God, Father, Son and Holy Spirit. This 'washing' had two meanings. It signified a cleansing away of the sins of the former manner of life, the new Christian emerging from the stream to be clothed in a white robe signifying his clean start. More profoundly, the candidate's disappearance into the deep and his re-emergence was seen as a way of personal identification with the death, burial, and resurrection of Jesus. As Paul wrote to the Romans:

> 'Have you forgotten that when we were baptized into union with Christ Jesus we were baptized into his death? By baptism we were buried with him, and lay dead, in order that, as Christ was raised from the dead in the splendour of the Father, so also we might set our feet upon the new path of life.'[2]

You can see that in the early days of the Christian Church Baptism was no mere naming ceremony, casual sprinkling, or social convention. It was an act of the utmost solemnity in which the new convert declared what it meant to him to say: 'I turn to Christ', and acknowledged his need of the power of God's Spirit and the encouragement of the Christian community to live up to the great obligations he had undertaken.

Adult readers of this book who are themselves preparing to be baptized will need no reminding of the great seriousness of the path they have determined to follow.

8

The ASB Baptism service will leave you in no doubt about this:

> 'Our Lord Jesus Christ suffered death on the cross and rose again from the dead for the salvation of mankind. Baptism is the outward sign by which we receive for ourselves what he has done for us; we are united with him in his death; we are granted the forgiveness of sins; we are raised with Christ to new life in the Spirit.
>
> Those of you who have come for baptism must affirm your allegiance to Christ and your rejection of all that is evil!'

This is followed by solemn questions and answers in which you declare your determination to turn to Christ by renouncing evil and repenting your sins and acknowledging that you believe and trust in God the Father, Son and Holy Spirit according to the faith of the Church. There is no doubt about the tremendous importance of these undertakings, and their meaning will be discussed in the following chapters.

As we have seen, only adults came for Baptism in the earliest years of the Christian Church. Some scholars think that in those days such importance was put on the family as a unit that if the head of the family were baptized, the children and other dependents would automatically be thought to have been incorporated into the fellowship of believers with him. But from at least as far back as the third century there has been an almost universal tradition that children born to Christian parents should be baptized in infancy. Although at the time of the Reformation a group of Protestant Churches insisted on a return to Baptism being only available to adult believers because that seems to have been the practice of earlier Christian congregations, the majority of

Churches, including the Church of England and others in the Anglican Communion, retained the practice of infant Baptism. Yet many people are today questioning this ancient tradition, because so many of those who bring their children to the font are only nominal Christians, with little or no link with their local church. The ASB Baptism service makes it absolutely clear that parents and godparents must make firm Christian affirmations not only on behalf of their children, but also for themselves.

I turn to Christ.

I repent of my sins.

I renounce evil.

They must 'declare before God and his Church the Christian faith into which your child is to be baptized, and in which you will help him to live and grow'. There is a strong debate in many Churches today on the necessity for a much stricter code of discipline in the administration of infant Baptism. It would make more sense, it is argued, if only those who were seriously committed to the faith and practice of the Church, should be allowed to bring their children to this solemn sacrament of initiation. Many clergy work hard to ensure that the teaching of the Church is understood and taken seriously by parents and godparents, insisting on some kind of preparation before they enter into these solemn obligations. Increasingly Baptism is administered in the course of normal Sunday worship so that it can be seen to be a sacrament of entry into the life of the Church, and not some private religious or even social occasion.

Most Christians believe that the ancient practice of infant Baptism should be retained as bearing witness to the essential truth that we are admitted into the family of Christ Jesus not on the strength of our own merits, but by an act of God's love. Just as in a human family we are born by the loving act of our parents, so in Baptism God declares to the child (and to his parents), 'This is my child'. The hope and prayer of the Christian family into which the child is baptized is that in due time he will learn to reply: 'You are my Father'.

Confirmation

The initiation into the life of the Christian Church which begins with Baptism is completed, in the Anglican tradition, by Confirmation and the receiving of Holy Communion. But what does Confirmation mean today? If Baptism is the effective means by which 'We are united with Christ in his death, granted the forgiveness of sins, and raised with Christ to new life in the Spirit', what else is there left for confirmation to do? One answer is that it is the way, after careful preparation of mind and heart we make our public response to Jesus Christ for what he has done for us. He has taken the initiative. It is now for us to accept his gift, and to be seen to be doing it. This can be one meaning of the word 'confirmation'. By this act we confirm the promises made by us, or on our behalf, at our Baptism. 'Those of you who come to be confirmed must with your own mouth and from your own heart declare your allegiance to Christ.'

But there is a deeper meaning. We come to Confirmation to ask for the strength we need to fulfil our desire to be faithful disciples of Christ. We know that we cannot achieve this on our own. We need the power for living which Jesus told his followers would come with the gift of the Spirit. From the earliest days the sign of trust that this promise would be fulfilled was the laying on of hands.[3] Not only in Confirmation, but in the

11

consecration of a bishop, at the ordination of a priest, and in many other kinds of commissioning, this is the outward sign. There is nothing magical about the laying on of hands. The bishop does not have a mystical supply of 'spirit' which he can pour out at will, rather like filling up a car at a petrol station. But Christians believe that when someone responds to the call of God to undertake a task which has been committed to him, he is given by the Holy Spirit the necessary power to do the job. Confirmation has been described as the ordination of the laity. No less than the bishop or the priest, the lay person has an appointed task in the life both of the Church and the world. No less than the bishop or priest, he needs to be ordained or commissioned to that task, and to be given the assurance that God will give him the power to fulfil faithfully what he has promised.

That assurance can be yours for the asking as you kneel before the bishop on your Confirmation day, and hear, as he lays his hands upon your head, those great words of confidence and trust: 'Confirm, O Lord, your servant with your Holy Spirit'.

FOR FURTHER THOUGHT AND DISCUSSION
ON INITIATION

1. Read Acts 2. 42-47.

   What does this tell you about the life of the Christian community in its earliest days?

   In what ways does it differ from what you know of the Church in our own day?

   How does this passage challenge your own personal life as a Christian?

2. Read Acts 9. 1-22.

What do you think were the factors which led to Paul's conversion?

Do you know anyone who has been converted in a similar way?

How did it happen?

What are the influences which have brought you to the decision to 'turn to Christ'?

3. Read Romans 6. 1-4.

If you were baptized in infancy, do you think this passage has any relevance for what took place then?

If you are preparing now for Baptism and/or Confirmation, what do these words say to you?

For your prayers.

Remember to pray
for the bishop who will confirm you;
for those who will be confirmed with you;
for your clergy and others helping you in your preparation.

You may like to use these prayers:

Lord God our Father
through our Saviour Jesus Christ
you have assured mankind of eternal life
and in baptism made us one with him.
Deliver us from the death of sin
and raise us to new life in your love
in the fellowship of the Holy Spirit
by the grace of our Lord Jesus Christ.   (ASB)

Heavenly Father, we bring to you in our prayers those who are preparing for confirmation. So work in our hearts by your Holy Spirit that we may be ready to receive all that you are seeking to teach us, and dedicate our lives to your service; and by your grace, keep us faithful to our promises all the days of our life; through Jesus Christ our Lord.

(Frank Colquhoun)

2. DISCIPLESHIP

School for disciples

There are three closely related episodes in the life of Jesus which show how he set about training his inner group of disciples to face the coming crisis. After a highly successful campaign of teaching and healing in the lovely countryside around the sea of Galilee, Jesus knew that the next stage of his mission would be more testing both for himself and for his disciples. The journey to Jerusalem would involve him in conflict and disappointment, for it was the road which led to Pilate's judgement hall, and to Calvary. Only after a careful programme of training would his closest followers have the courage and vision to remain faithful to him, and to carry on his work in a hostile world after his crucifixion and resurrection. This training in discipleship for a time of crisis is described in three episodes which Matthew, Mark and Luke all narrate in some detail.[4] The theme of these three events is:

> The questioning which leads to commitment.
> The worship which leads to reassurance.
> The action which leads to faith.

These three stories provide a firm basis for the training of men and women preparing to assume full membership of the Church today.

The first story begins with a conversation between

Jesus and his disciples as they walk along the road together. He asked them what the general public was saying about him. The invitation to gossip about other people's funny ideas was eagerly accepted. They told him that people had the craziest theories about him. Some folk said that he was John the Baptist come to life again, others believed he was Elijah whom popular tradition said would return to earth at the end of the world. Yet others heard it rumoured that he might be Jeremiah or one of the other prophets. In matters of religion, as in much else, it is always easy to poke fun at the mad opinions of other people. But Jesus cut short the gossip about other people and their ideas with the direct question: 'You — who do you say that I am?' Of course, we have to rely on getting our ideas about God second-hand from other people. We may have been profoundly influenced by a priest or a trusted friend, or the words we hear on the radio, or ideas derived from Billy Graham or the Pope. More especially the words of the Bible and the Prayer Book shape our picture of God. But the moment comes when we have to answer, for ourselves and in our own words, the greatest of all questions: 'Who do you say that I am?' And when an adult comes forward for Baptism or Confirmation, the moment to face that great question has arrived. Matthew tells us that Peter replied immediately with the greatest affirmation: 'You are the Son of the living God'. Did he know what he was saying? At that time Peter can have only vaguely understood the full meaning of the words which came so quickly to his lips. This is true of all of us. We go to church, say the creeds and join in the prayers set down for us. But how little we can really understand what we repeat with so little thought. The whole of our Christian life must be a process of exploration and discovery as we come, little by little, to grasp more of the meaning of the tremendous things we say.

We have to learn not only the meaning of the words we use, but also their practical implication for our own lives. As soon as Peter had answered the Lord's challenge, Jesus spoke of the suffering which would be the fate of all those who followed him to the end. 'If anyone wishes to be a disciple of mine, he must leave self behind: he must take up his cross and come with me.' It is the easiest thing in the world to stand up in the church and sing to a comfortably familiar tune:

> Take up thy cross, the Saviour said,
> If thou would'st my disciple be;
> Deny thyself, the world forsake,
> And humbly follow after me.

But dare any of us face up to what it is we are singing in that much loved hymn? A distinguished American scholar has said that when Jesus told his disciples that they must 'take up their cross' this was 'no easy platitude of the spiritual life. The modern reader can easily dissolve the iron into cobwebs, but those who wrote and first read the gospels could not, for the language reminded them too harshly of the criminal courts and the prison cell.' Those of us for whom it is comparatively easy to make a public witness to Christ have to remember that for many of our fellow Christians in other parts of the world to do this is to take up a cross. Can you ask yourself what personal cost you would be prepared to pay for the privilege of Baptism and Confirmation if it were demanded of you?

So the roadside conversation which began with easy gossip about the foibles of other people's silly opinions led the disciples to face the most demanding choice of their lives — to go forward with him or to stay behind.

17

This choice comes to all of us when our interest in religion moves from being a discussion *about* God to becoming a personal encounter *with* God. And the demands that this encounter makes might be far from comfortable for any of us.

This episode must have left the disciples bewildered and frightened. Would following Jesus to Jerusalem really have such fearful consequences? They were in desperate need of reassurance, and this came six days later when Jesus took the three who were closest to him up the mount of transfiguration to see him in a wonderful vision 'shining like the sun'. It was a heartwarming experience of the glory of God, and Peter once again voiced the feeling of them all when he exclaimed, 'Lord, how good it is that we are here'. If the decision to follow Jesus makes many heavy demands on us, both in the way we think and in the way we live our daily lives, worship can bring us the reassurance we need. Discipleship raises many questions for the sensitive intelligent Christian. Worship can bring the same sort of confidence in the trustworthiness of God as a man and woman feel when they fall in love and dare to make life-long commitment to one another in marriage.

This must have been the experience of Peter, James and John as they saw the transfigured Christ. They knew that the reply they gave to Jesus by the roadside was true when they dared to say, 'You are the Son of the living God'. What they had worked out in discussion walking along the road was now ratified on their knees on the mountain top.

'It was not on tales artfully spun that we relied when we told you of the power of our Lord Jesus Christ and his coming; we saw him with our own eyes in majesty, when at the hands of God the

Father he was invested with honour and majesty.'[5]

So in the course of training for meeting the crisis ahead, Jesus began with the challenge of himself (Who do you say that I am?), and then went on to give an assurance of the glory of God in the experience of prayer and worship. Those who decide to commit themselves to Christ (You are the living God), must then discover on their knees the assurance which worship brings. (It is good for us to be here.) In particular Christians know that they meet their Lord in the Eucharist when, as they receive the bread and wine, they affirm that they are eating and drinking these holy gifts in the presence of the divine majesty.

But there is a third section in this training course which must be taken as seriously as the call to faith and worship. It is the call to service. The three apostles obviously so much enjoyed the vision on the mountain top that they would have been content to stay there forever. This is probably what Peter had in mind when in the excitement of the moment he blurted out that strange remark about building three shelters. But it was not the intention of Jesus that they should spend the rest of their lives prostrate before the vision of glory. There was work to be done on earth, and worship must never become a means of escape from facing up to the harsh challenges of daily life. As soon as Peter had suggested building shelters the clouds came down and the vision faded. The three disciples found themselves walking down the mountain with Jesus telling them what lay ahead. The Lord who had been seen in glory had now to suffer the humble realities of trial, mockery and death. True discipleship is costly. For Jesus it was more costly than for anyone else because in his sinlessness he had to bear the sins of the whole world. Already at the foot of the mountain the disciples were brought face to face with the dark side of life. They came upon a tragic little crowd. An anxious father, some of the followers of Jesus helpless and bewildered, and the usual group of onlookers who always appear when there is an incident. In the centre a boy was lying on the ground seized with an uncontrollable fit. Luke, with his interest in medical matters, gives a graphic description of the symptoms in the words of the lad's father: 'From time to time a spirit seizes him, gives a sudden scream, and throws him into convulsions with foaming at the mouth, and it keeps on mauling him and will hardly let him go'.[6] It is tempting to see in this graphic picture an image of what we have to return to as we come out of the uplifting experience of our Sunday worship to face the world again. The nuclear arms race, industrial unrest, broken marriage, racism, world poverty, international terrorism, crime and violence, alcohol and drug addiction, political wrangling all suggest a world out of control. A spirit seizes us again and again in our dealings with one another, throwing us into convulsions, mauling us, and hardly letting us go. Like the disciples in the story, we look at the influences of evil in our distracted world and exclaim 'Why can we not cast it out?' Luke tells us that Jesus cured the boy, and handed him back to his father. He then adds a significant comment: 'They were all struck with awe at the majesty of God.' Christ, who had revealed himself in conversation with his disciples, and on the mountain top vision, now reveals God's awe-inspiring majesty when an epileptic boy is brought back to health by his healing touch. The glory of God is revealed whenever the followers of Jesus Christ have faith that divine love can act in the face of a deranged world and are prepared to go into action to prove it. When the challenges of life become too strong and the fight against evil too unequal, it is tempting for the Christian to run up the mountain to find an escape in the satisfaction of worship. But just as commitment to Christ inevitably leads us to worship, so worship must compel us to face the real problems of life, armed with the assurance of his love and power. Here is the threefold cord of discipleship: faith, worship, service. And this is the threefold commitment in the service of Christ to which those who come to Baptism and Confirmation are called.

Believing and trusting

In the Confirmation service those who are to be confirmed, together with the whole congregation, make an act of faith.

> This is our faith.
> We believe and trust in one God
> Father, Son, and Holy Spirit.

Peter urged his readers to be 'always ready with your defence whenever you are called to account for the hope that is in you'.[7] People are not usually won to the Christian Church solely by intellectual argument, but this does not excuse adult Christians who apply some intelligence to their daily work or leisure interests, from bringing their brains as well as their feelings to bear upon the faith they profess. How do Christians come to believe in the things they say and sing about God in the creeds, hymns and prayers of the Church? Do these things stand up to intellectual examination in these scientific days, or is it all a matter of guessing and wishful thinking?

Part of your preparation for Confirmation must be your willingness to come to grips with these questions as honestly and as intelligently as you can. You cannot hope to persuade others of the faith which is in you unless you are yourself convinced that it is based on firm foundations. We may not be able to prove (or disprove) that God exists in the way that we can deal with a problem in mathematics or physics. Ultimately, for the follower of Christ, proof comes from experience rather than from argument. But this does not mean that our Christian faith is superstitious or irrational. There are valid reasons for being a Christian today as at any other time in history. How do we discover them?

The questions to the candidates for Baptism and Confirmation are carefully phrased.

> Do you believe and trust in God the Father, who made the world?

> Do you believe and trust in his Son, Jesus Christ, who redeemed mankind?

> Do you believe and trust in the Holy Spirit, who gives life to the people of God?

To each of these three questions you will answer: 'I believe and trust.' Note those two words — believe and trust. Belief means taking hold of the facts which describe the way that God has made himself known to us. Trust means taking those facts seriously as the guiding inspiration for our daily lives. Discipleship involves both believing in God and trusting in him. Belief without trust can be a mere intellectual exercise. Trust without belief can be a naive delusion. When you say that you believe and trust in God, you are making the most far-reaching declaration of your life.

But from where do we get these facts about God upon which we can surely base our belief and trust? This is a question we need to explore. We can begin by looking at ourselves. As far as we know, man in the only animal who asks questions about himself. Your cat (if you have one) is content with his cattiness. Because you are human, you are restless, enquiring, exploring, aware, sometimes joyfully but often painfully, of the world of which you are a part and yet from which, in some ways, you feel aloof. Are there not moments when standing under the night sky, or in the loneliness of your room, you find yourself asking why you are here and what is the meaning of life? Why do you instinctively appreciate beauty, courage, self-sacrifice and love? Why do you know that love is not just to do with sex or self-gratification but has a much more profound meaning for which you are always searching? Why does truth matter so much that you are shocked when people in public life tell lies, or men are imprisoned in totalitarian countries for telling the truth as they see it. Is the answer to these questions simply to be found, as some people tell us, in the way we are made, physically or mentally, in our economic or social situation, or because deep down we are all frightened and lonely and must invent gods to give ourselves comfort and assurance? There is some truth in all this. The way we are made and the kind of people we are does have some influence on the way we face life. Economic and social conditions can colour our religious outlook as they certainly colour our political thinking. We all have moments of fear and loneliness when we are glad that we have a religious faith to give us courage and companionship. There is no need to feel ashamed to confess that all these things may be factors in our search for God. But they cannot provide the full answer. If a person experiences love, beauty, truth and goodness believing them to matter so much that they are worth living and dying for, can we be satisfied with the explanation which says that this is simply the way we happen to be made? Human beings are not run by computers or wound up by clock-work. When you say with complete confidence:

I know that is beautiful;
I really love that person;
I am convinced that this is true;
that person is good;
that would be worth dying for;

may it not be that you are responding to an influence which comes from outside yourself, as a transistor radio picks up programmes which do not originate from inside it? Only the cynic who refuses to believe because he does not want to believe can say that the only possible motive for being honest in business is the fear of being found out and sent to prison, or the only thing that prevents a man from going to bed with a prostitute is the fear of contracting disease, or that the only reason why people trust in God is a weak-kneed fear of life. Are not amongst the most courageous human beings today those who have the deepest religious faith, such as Mother Teresa of Calcutta and Bishop Desmond Tutu of South Africa? If you cannot prove the existence of God, you certainly cannot simply explain him away.

What equipment have we been given with which to build up our faith? We have our natural ability to ask questions, to use our reason, and to appreciate beauty. We also have our consciences which provide us with an elementary (though not always reliable) guide to right and wrong. All these faculties should be used in our explorations as fully and as honestly as we can. But we need more certain guidance. This we must find in the pages of the Bible, and in the witness of those Christians who have gone before us and left us the creeds and many other testimonies to faith. In our pilgrimage we are surrounded by a great cloud of witnesses.

The first of those witnesses were the disciples who knew Jesus Christ face to face, and who, together with those who were immediately influenced by them, formed a community of men and women who experienced a new kind of living because of the life, teaching, death and resurrection of Jesus Christ. The Christian Church began neither with the Bible nor with statements of faith such as the creeds, but with a living community convinced that God had revealed himself to mankind in a more complete and decisive way than ever before. A first hand account of what that experience meant can be found in the letters which Paul and others wrote to the earliest local gatherings of Christians, and in the stories, memories and meditations on the life of Jesus as eyewitnesses recalled them, which came to be written down later in the four gospels. It was not until three hundred years after the time of Jesus that all these writings were collected together into the single volume we now call the New Testament. This was added to the Jewish Scriptures of the Law and the Prophets (The Old Testament) on which the first Christians, who were Jews, had been nourished. So the Holy Bible came into being. For the Christian, the Bible is the unique (though not the only) guide to the way God has made himself known all down history. Because God is the same yesterday, today and forever, this book is rightly claimed not only to be a tale of 'once upon a time', but a source of inspiration for all time for those who want to know how God makes himself known not only in personal experiences, but in the ups and downs of social, national and international events.

The Bible is not always an easy book to read, but the remarkable fact about it is that in spite of the length of time between the earliest and the latest of its writings, and the diversity of the events described, a consistent picture emerges. It is the one and the same God who is revealed in the life stories of Abraham, Moses, Amos, Hosea and Isaiah, by the writers of the Psalms and the Genesis creation stories, in the chronicles of the early Christian Church and above all in the life of Jesus of Nazareth. It is the same God who speaks from beginning to end, though his voice is not heard with equal clarity in every part of the Bible. But the more we allow the scholars to tell us about the cultural, historical and religious backgrounds of each writer, illuminating why he wrote what he did, what audience he had in mind, and what he was trying to say, the more clearly emerges this powerful impression that behind these pages the living God is at work, making his purposes known for the benefit of all mankind through the story of a small insignificant nation in the Middle East over a period of about two thousand years of history. It may be misleading to speak of the Bible as the Word of God, but it can be said of the words of Scripture, as of no other collection of writings, that they give clear evidence that God has spoken to men and women of successive generations through the life story of one particular nation. It is because in these pages we believe that we can hear the authentic voice of God that we dare to speak of the Bible as inspired. That is why you will not progress along the Christian way without making the study of the Bible a very important part of your life. But you will need help in understanding it. Fortunately there is much good material available today to enable you to do this.

FOR FURTHER THOUGHT AND DISCUSSION
ON DISCIPLESHIP

1. Read Matthew 16. 13-28.

If Jesus asked you, 'Who do men say that I am?',
how would you answer in the light of your knowledge of other people's views about him?

If he asked you, 'Who do you say that I am?', how
would you answer, giving your honest thoughts and
not just what you think you might be expected to
say?

2. Read Matthew 17. 1-13;
   also Exodus 33. 18-23, Ezekiel 1. 26-28, Isaiah 6. 1-9.
   In the light of these passages, do you think we fail to
   give due emphasis to the majesty of God both in
   public worship and in our personal prayers?

   We use the word 'glory' frequently in worship. How
   would you define it?

3. Read Matthew 17. 19-20.
   Is it really true? If not, what do you think Jesus
   meant?

For your prayers.

Pray for your continual exploration to find an
answer to the question, 'Who do you say that I am?'

Pray for a deeper sense of the majesty of God.

You may like to use this prayer:

Lord Jesus Christ, who appeared in majesty to your
disciples on the mountain and spoke of your coming
passion; we adore you in the glory of your transfiguration and own you as our crucified Lord; and
we pray that we, beholding and reflecting your
glory, may be changed into your likeness from one
degree of glory to another by the Lord the Spirit, to
the praise and honour of your name.

(Frank Colquhoun)

3. BELIEF

The Father

'Do you believe and trust in God the Father who made the world?' This is the first of the great truths you will affirm on your confirmation day. It is a truth with which both the Bible and the creeds begin.

'We believe in one God, the Father, the almighty, maker of heaven and earth, of all that is seen and unseen.'

The first book of the Old Testament tells us, in stories of incomparable beauty, of the beginnings of the universe, and of human life. We do not go to these chapters to find a scientific account of the origin of things. If we want that kind of information we will find up-to-date scientific books in our nearest public library. But the Genesis stories tell us something quite unique, and even more important. They tell us in magnificent story form, that God himself was in action in the creation of the universe, and how he has continued to be in action in the progress of history and the affairs of mankind. We can call these stories myths, legends or parables if we so wish. What we cannot say is that they are not true. For they provide a powerful introduction to one of the main themes of our Christian faith. They assure us that the world and everything in it depends upon God for its existence, whereas God depends on nothing outside himself. They provide the assurance, which later was to form an essential part of the teaching of Jesus Christ himself, that despite defeats and disasters, life is not meaningless. The world is ordered and reliable, because God created it and continues to sustain it. The only blot on the landscape is human disobedience.

Some of the finest passages in the Old Testament are poems in praise of the creator God. Read in a good modern translation Psalm 104, or Isaiah 40. 21-31. Turn to the book of Job which is a kind of dramatic discussion on the problem of the suffering of an innocent man. If you read the whole book you may not think that it provides an entirely satisfactory answer to the question it is trying to deal with. But if you read from the beginning of chapter 38 to chapter 41 verse 34, you are likely to find the author's picture of God's power over the created world breathtakingly exciting.

Many people have found faith in God the Father who made the world by looking at the marvellous intricacy and pattern of the natural order. Isaac Newton, the most eminent scientist of the seventeenth century described his work as 'thinking God's thoughts after him'. Natural historians and chemists at that time were usually deeply religious people, seeing the hand of God in all their researches. The eighteenth century poet Joseph Addison expressed this optimistic view of creation in a beautiful hymn which is still sometimes sung:

The spacious firmament on high,
With all the blue ethereal sky,
And spangled heavens, a shining frame,
Their great Original proclaim.
The unwearied sun from day to day
Does his Creator's power display,
And publishes to every land

The work of an almighty hand.

This was very typical of Anglican thinking three hundred years ago. Today we are tempted to take a less romantic view and to speak, as Tennyson did, of 'nature red in tooth and claw'. We are puzzled by the apparent cruelty of much that happens in the natural world in the struggle for survival. The children's hymn celebrates 'all things bright and beautiful all creatures great and small', and declares that the 'Lord God made them all'. Does this include the tapeworm, the head louse, or the bacteria of cholera or typhus? How does the generally accepted theory of evolution square with the Bible picture of creation? Some scientists find it hard to 'believe and trust in God the Father who made the world'. The evidence derived from their laboratory and field studies does not lead them to this conclusion. If God is good, how can all these things be explained? But other scholars, in the field of both religion and science, have seen the struggle in the world of nature as a kind of travail towards new birth as God continues to carry out his creative purposes. They find modern theories of evolution reflected in the Bible, as in a remarkable passage in the letter which Paul wrote to the Christians in Rome.

> 'We know the whole created universe groans in all its parts as if in the pangs of childbirth ... even we, to whom the Spirit is given as first fruits of the harvest to come, are groaning inwardly while we wait for God to make us his sons and set our whole body free.'[8]

Here we are moving into deep waters, not easy to fathom. It is no good pretending that we can find easy answers to these questions. But it can be said with confidence that when you come to affirm that you believe and trust in God the Father who made the world, you are not saying something which flies in the face of modern thought. Some scientists will not agree with you (neither will a great many other people). But many will. You can hold fast to your faith in a creator God.

But we have to take this act of faith a stage further. It is easy to think of God as some kind of electric current or computer system ticking away behind the universe. The Bible insists in speaking of God in personal terms. God is he, not it. This is not to say that God is *a* person in the normal sense of the word. This would be to fall into the trap of making God in our own image. When we speak of our belief in a personal God, we mean to say that our relationship with the deity is not like that of a man to an electronic system, but the kind of relationship human beings expect to have with one another. Our relationship with him is with person, and not with thing. This is the teaching of the Bible from the beginning to the end. 'The Lord', it is said 'would speak with Moses face to face, as one man speaks with another.'[9] The Psalmist wrote:

'As a father has compassion on his children,
So has the Lord compassion on all who fear him.'[10]

Hosea dares to put these tender words into the mouth of God:

'When Israel was a boy, I loved him;
I called my son out of Egypt;
but the more I called, the further they went from me'.[11]

Isaiah was even more bold, likening God's relationship with his chosen people to that of husband and wife. 'Your husband is your maker who is the Lord of hosts.'[12]

So it is that Jesus taught his disciples to pray to God as Father, and the word he used, Abba, was the familiar affectionate address of a child to his parents.

Yet we always have to be on our guard against

belittling God by the language we use about him. We are only able to speak of him in terms that reflect our human experience. We say that he is like a father, a husband, a judge, a shepherd, a king. But these are picture words drawn from our experience here on earth. God is greater than any human language we can use about him. That is why the ancient Jews were forbidden to make images of God, or even to pronounce his name, for fear that they might be treating him as a mere human. If we dare to call God our Father (as Jesus taught us to do) and use earthly language about him, we have also to keep in mind the other side of the picture, that God is totally other.

> Immortal, invisible, God only wise,
> In light inaccessible, hid from our eyes,
> Most blessed, most glorious, the Ancient of Days,
> Almighty, victorious, thy great name we praise.

This is a paradox, but it is important to try to grasp it. Yet God has not left us with this conundrum to grope in the dark. He who is 'light inaccessible hid from our eyes' has also revealed himself as fully as is possible on the human scene in the life of Jesus of Nazareth.

Jesus Christ

When you affirm that you believe and trust in Jesus Christ who redeemed mankind you are committing yourself to the central core of the Christian gospel. Others may believe in God as creator. Only Christians acknowledge Jesus Christ as Lord and saviour. What does this mean, and what is the evidence?

In about the year 112 the governor of the Roman province of Bithynia (the Black Sea district) wrote to the Emperor Trajan raising a question which was puzzling him. Should this tiresome new movement called the Christians be suppressed because they were probably an illegal organization, or must they be charged with some specific crime. He described their activities. 'It is their habit on a fixed day to assemble before daylight and to recite by turns a form of words to Christ as God. The contagion of this perverse and extravagant superstition has penetrated not the cities only, but the villages and the country. Yet it still seems possible to stop it.'

Not long afterwards somebody in Rome drew an anti-Christian cartoon. It was a picture, painted on a wall, of a crucifix on which hung a figure with a head like that of a donkey. Another figure is pictured kneeling beside it. Below is the caption 'Alexamenos worships his god'. We should not be surprised to get this evidence of public reaction of this kind. To the outsider Christianity must have seemed a very odd religion. Who were these strange people propagating their faith in a crucified god and claiming that they had not only found a new understanding of God because of Jesus Christ, but were experiencing a new way to God through him? And who was this Jesus Christ? He was a Jewish village carpenter who had left his trade to become a wandering preacher, had found himself in conflict with the authorities and had been executed by the Romans as a terrorist. And yet his followers were now beginning to call him Lord and Son of God, deriving new hope, new courage and new power because of him. This new religion must have seemed (as Paul claimed it would) stupid, blasphemous, and dangerous to the sophisticated Greeks, the devout Jews and the clever Romans.[13]

Christianity is now nearly two thousand years old, and most of you who read this book will have been brought up in a Christian country and educated in the Christian tradition. So we have come to take for granted a faith which makes such extravagant claims about a man who lived once upon a time. The first letter we have from the pen of Paul was written just twenty years after the death of Jesus. It includes this remarkable statement: 'We believe that Jesus Christ died and rose again; and so it will be for those who die as Christians; God will bring them to life with Jesus.'[14]

Jesus Christ not only ranks as one of the great world figures in the story of religion and thought, along with Moses, the Buddha, Socrates, Confucius and Mohammed. He plays a part in Christianity occupied by no other religious founder. Christianity is not *about* Jesus. Christianity *is* Jesus. Here is our key to an understanding of the Christian life. A Christian is not just someone who tries to be a good neighbour or is 'against sin'. A Christian is someone who finds the focus of his understanding of God and his relationship with God in Jesus Christ. That is what you will mean when you say, 'I believe and trust in Jesus Christ who redeemed mankind'.

But how can we come to know about Jesus so that we may believe and trust in him? Our only evidence of his life are the stories, traditions and memories put together by eyewitnesses and others during the first century after his death. The stories told by Matthew, Mark, Luke and John in their gospels are a mixture of accurate reporting, legend and pious meditation. They are not biographies in the modern sense of the word. Many of the things we would like to know about him are not included. We do not know exactly when he was born, and even the stories of his birth (in Matthew and Luke) are confusing. Except for one incident, we know nothing of his life from his birth until he was thirty years old. The gospel writers concentrated on the final two and a half years when we have a fairly detailed description of his work and travels in a small Middle East country about the size of Wales. It is his teaching and his style of life which comes out most clearly in these accounts. He took sides with the misunderstood and the underprivileged, with the sick in mind and body, with foreign soldiers, prostitutes, aliens and all those who were considered second class citizens. He had, in Bishop David Sheppard's phrase, a 'bias to the poor'. He seems to have been scornful of rank, wealth, power and pretentiousness. He taught about God and man by telling unconventional stories, drawing his illustrations from everyday life rather than from 'churchy' things. He was the least moralistic of great religious teachers, being, for example, less critical of a woman caught in the very act of adultery than he was of the moral majority who wanted to stone her to death on the spot. He did not lay down a detailed code of rules and regulations (he was accused of being a law breaker), but taught his followers a number of shining principles such as love, honesty, integrity, humility and self sacrifice upon which all moral decisions must be based. And he insisted that his teaching about God and life had to be translated into down-to-earth action here and now. This action he called 'the kingdom of God', and by his teaching and by his miracles he demonstrated what this kingdom would be like when men and women allowed the rule of God to direct their individual and community lives. He taught his disciples to pray daily that his kingdom might come on earth. His gospel was not an appeal to be other worldly. His concern was that God's will should be done here and now.

As opposition to his teaching mounted both from the political and ecclesiastical authorities, he displayed within himself an increasing serenity and confidence which was seen to come from his obvious closeness to God. He himself claimed to have a special relationship when he said 'If you have seen me, you have seen the Father'. This could have seemed a very big-headed claim if it were not for the fact that Jesus was the least proud among men. But sheer goodness always poses a threat to those in power — to big business, to political ambition, even to the organized Church. So Jesus was branded as a blasphemer by the church of his day and as a threat to political stability by the leaders of the state. He was arrested, tried and executed by crucifixion, the normal method of carrying out the death penalty for those guilty of terrorism.

So Jesus was killed on the cross. And yet in a matter of hours his followers were convinced that God's purposes had not been checkmated. On the contrary, they were talking not about the defeat of Jesus but of his victory. Their watchword became, Jesus lives! As we read the first available records of the life of the Christian community twenty years or so after the crucifixion, we find that they are not speaking of Jesus as the memory of a man now dead, but as the living continuous presence of a real person. In the Acts of the Apostles and the epistles there is hardly any reference at all to the details of the earthly life of Jesus. He is always there in the present tense, not in the past. He is God's final word to man, they are saying. Believe in him and you will find a new quality of living. This is Christianity.

The resurrection of Jesus is central to our faith. Every book in the New Testament assumes that 'on the third day he rose again'. Christians claim that this is no myth, but a fact of history. But can we believe it really happened? What is the evidence? The earliest account we have comes from Paul. The apostle was not himself an eyewitness of the events he describes, but he mentions the sources from which he received his information, like Peter who 'saw and believed'.[15] The gospel accounts come later and in different ways fill in the details. But it is not easy at this distance of time to know exactly what happened that first Easter morning. Whilst many people are content to accept all the evidence as 'gospel' (the angels, the rolled away stone, the grave clothes and the empty tomb), other may want to be more open-minded about the literal truth of all these details. What cannot be explained away is the extraordinary transformation among the followers of Jesus who on Good Friday 'all forsook him and fled', but who not many weeks later were proclaiming the resurrection with boldness and conviction in the very city where the crucifixion had taken place. 'You used heathen men to crucify and kill him. But God raised him to life again, setting him free from the pangs of death, because it could not be that death should keep him in its grip.'[16]

Such profound conviction, and the courage to face persecution and death because of it, could not have been based on wishful thinking alone. All the evidence points to an event on Easter morning which convinced the eyewitnesses, and those who heard their testimony, that Jesus had overcome death and was alive. Through prayer and sacrament, and in obeying his command to preach this gospel and spread the kingdom, they knew for sure that his presence was with them. This is the faith in which countless Christians have lived all down the centuries, and to which you will bear witness on your confirmation day.

In your reply to the bishop's question, you will focus your belief in Jesus as the one who came into the world to redeem mankind. What does that mean? Thousands of people have been killed for their beliefs. Some have died deaths more horrible and painful than Jesus did, and have shown equal courage. What is so special about the death of this man? The answer comes in some words of Paul written not many years after the crucifixion. 'God offered him so that by his death he should become the means by which people's sins are forgiven.'[17] This is the language of sacrifice, and it came to be an important part of Christian thinking as it had been for the Jews in Old Testament times. The first disciples had been brought up in the Jewish sacrificial tradition. Sacrifices were offered in the temple to wash away (or atone for) sin, and to restore (or redeem) the communion between God and his people which human sin had shattered. So, in the Holy Communion service in the Book of Common Prayer, the prayer of consecration speaks of Christ's death upon the cross 'for our redemption; who made there, by his one oblation of himself once offered, a full, perfect, and sufficient sacrifice, oblation and satisfaction for the sins of the whole world'. It was natural that the first Christians, feeling an overwhelming sense of release from their sins and joy at their experience of freedom, should use the familiar language of sacrifice to express their new found faith in the saving power of Christ.

Whenever we talk about God and his dealings with us we must always remember the limitations of human language. All down the centuries scholars and preachers have tried to find, with varying success, words with which to speak of the power of Christ crucified to bring new life to sinful mankind. Many of these words have become familiar to us in hymns, prayers and the Bible itself. If you commit yourself to Christ, you must become familiar with the language of his Church.

But the words and images we use to describe Christian

experience have to be treated with caution. They can be a help to our understanding, or they can lead us into appalling misunderstanding. For instance some have said that man's new relationship with God became possible because Jesus offered himself to the Father as a sacrificial lamb, a ransom for our sins. The picture has valuable lessons to teach. The sacrificial lamb was costly, not easy for a poor family to provide. The atonement for sin is costly. There is no cheap grace available. Even in human relationships self-sacrifice is considered the supreme act of practical love and compassion. How much more powerful when the sacrificial victim is the sinless Jesus, dying on a cross for the sake of his friends. Yet we have to be careful not to carry the picture too far. The idea of a God who needs a costly gift in order to appease his anger is far removed from the picture of God in the story of the prodigal son.

Or there is the concept of satisfaction. Just as a man must pay a big fine to be liberated from imprisonment, so God demanded a high price if man is to be freed from the bondage of sin.

'There was no other good enough
To pay the price of sin
He only could unlock the gate
Of heaven, and let us in.'

Again this emphasizes the seriousness of sin and the cost of redemption. But carried too literally it fails to do justice to the overwhelming generosity of God's love.

Some have talked of Christ as our substitute. In its crudest form it suggests that the Father sent the Son to be punished in our place. This makes us feel bound to ask what kind of God it is who arranges things that they have to be like that. Yet such phrases as 'Christ died for me' are a powerful stimulus to devotion, as men look at

39

the cross and see Christ willingly offering himself on their behalf. The noble substitute at the scaffold or in face of disaster has been a recurring theme in literature, and always evokes an admiring response in the reader. A similar picture is that of salvation, and the word 'saved' has been commonly (and often very superficially) used to explain the experience of being rescued from a situation from which we could not possibly extricate ourselves.

Paul reached the heart of the matter in a sentence which speaks more eloquently about the atoning work of Christ than any other statement of Scripture.

> 'Christ was without sin, but for our sake God made him share our sin in order that in union with him we might share the righteousness of God.'[18]

What he is saying is this; Jesus is the most complete picture of God in flesh and blood that it is possible to imagine. At the crisis moment of his earthly life he hangs on a cross with two convicted sinners on either side of him. Here is the sign that God is totally identified with humanity. Sin is the yawning gap which separates man from God, and which man by himself cannot bridge. But here God in Christ spans that gap by himself filling the place of separation. Here, when man thought that he must be most estranged from God, is Jesus making available to his followers the completely unmerited friendliness of God. Nothing, says Paul, can separate us from the love of God now that Christ himself has filled the gap and provided the bridge. Trouble, hardship, persecution, hunger, poverty, danger, death. In all these things we have complete victory. And that victory is not ours because we have earned it, because of our own piety or good works, because we are holier than other people. It is there because of God's overwhelming and generous love.[19] Good works, piety, devotion are not the coins by which we pay for our share of redemption. They are the signs of the genuineness of our response.

When on the eve of passion Jesus prayed to his Father for his disciples whom he was soon to leave, he said: 'This is eternal life: to know thee who art truly God, and Jesus Christ whom thou hast sent.'[20] So he taught, through his life, death and resurrection, that eternal life is not just something we may hope for beyond death. It is available to us here and now through the knowledge and experience of God which comes to us because of what Jesus has done for us. And because he has promised to be with us always, we know that even death cannot destroy that relationship by separating us from God's love.

The only separation can be of our own making, our persistence in sin, and our refusal to accept his gift of forgiveness. What happens when we die remains a mystery. But we know from the teaching of Jesus that God is infinitely merciful. We know that he takes sin seriously. These two complementary truths of the mercy and the judgement of God are expressed in the traditional concepts of heaven and hell. These are useful symbols of the reality of God's love and the seriousness of our disobedience. But they are only pictures, and we must not embroider details of a situation about which, at our stage of existence, we cannot know.

The creeds, following the teaching of the New Testament, speak of the resurrection of the body. Many people are puzzled by this. There was a time when people used to imagine bodies (often fully clothed), rising out of their graves on the resurrection day. Pictures of this happening were popular in many Victorian households, and they hold a certain period charm and fascination. But today it is less easy to think like that. It is right that you should continue to express your belief in the resurrection of the body when you join in the creeds, provided you know what it is you are trying to say. You are trying to make clear that whatever else we may think about the future life, it is not to be imagined as the realm of ghosts, shades, disembodied spirits, or spiritual birds released from the imprisonment of their earthly cages. On the contrary, just as the spirit of man is expressed here on earth only through his body, so in a future state, far from being less real and less recognizable (as a ghost is) it will express itself as Paul told the Corinthians in the kind of body appropriate to a new mode of existence. Obviously we are no longer talking of body in physical terms. We are simply saying that we believe that beyond the grave a person is more of a person than he ever was before. Behind the Church's teaching about the resurrection of the body lies the conviction, not of some grotesque physical resuscitation, but of the continuing personal identity of the whole man.[21]

Throughout Christian history there have been many wonderful testimonies to the assurance of victory which the resurrection of Jesus has given to men and women as they pass from this life to the next. Few are more moving than the words of Pastor Dietrich Bonhoeffer, the German theologian, who in 1945, as the warders came to fetch him from his cell in a Nazi concentration camp and to take him to his place of execution, turned to one of his fellow prisoners, an English army officer, and said: 'This is the end. For me it is the beginning of life.'[22]

Holy Spirit

There remains one more statement of faith which you are required to make as you commit yourself to full membership of Christ and his Church. You must affirm that

42

you believe and trust in the Holy Spirit who gives life to the people of God. It is important that you understand what this means, for the gift of the Spirit is an integral part of both Baptism and Confirmation. For those to be baptized the prayer is offered that God will 'send his Holy Spirit upon them to bring them to new birth in the family of the Church'. At your Confirmation the bishop prays that you may be confirmed with the Holy Spirit and that you may daily increase in that Holy Spirit more and more. Christians speak of God as Father, Son and Holy Spirit. Whatever words we use about God we know that we are attempting to describe a mystery far beyond the capacity of human language. Yet the picture of God as Father has some meaning for us because parenthood is part of our own experience. And when we speak of the Son, we know that we are talking about the God who revealed himself to us as the Jesus of the Gospels. But the idea of the Holy Spirit seems much more difficult to grasp. We can understand such a phrase as 'the spirit of Jesus' because we talk (for example) of the Boy Scouts following the spirit of their founder. But the concept of the Holy Spirit as a distinct and separate 'person' is much less easy to comprehend. Christian belief in the Holy Spirit emerged out of the growing experience of the guidance of God and the nearness of Christ as the infant Church moved forward in size and influence. Jesus had promised that they would experience God's Spirit, and events proved that the promise had been abundantly fulfilled. The Acts of the Apostles can be described as the gospel of the Holy Spirit.

The Nicene Creed speaks of the Holy Spirit as the giver of life. This was the experience of the first Christians. Through the inspiration of the Spirit they found themselves in possession of new powers which enabled them to live their lives with a courage and determination which they were convinced were gifts from God. Yet such a vision of divine activity was not entirely new. There are many references to the work of the Spirit of God in the Old Testament, and they are relevant in our attempts today to interpret the Christian doctrine of the Spirit's activity. The Hebrew word for Spirit used in the book of Genesis and elsewhere means breath. The Spirit of God is the life of God. God bestows life upon us by breathing his Spirit into us. 'Breathe on me breath of God, fill me with life anew.' It represents the outgoing activity of God.

Already at the end of the Old Testament the Spirit had been seen as God's activity displayed in human endeavour, in artistry and craftsmanship, in physical strength, in leadership, in ecstasy, in the interpretation of political and social events, in the pursuit of knowledge, in concern for human welfare, and in the hopes for a future in which mankind will enjoy peace and brotherhood. The New Testament takes hold of these ideas, develops them and gives them sharper focus.

If the Spirit is the outgoing activity of God, then Jesus must have been 'spirit filled'. And this is the picture the four Gospels give. His coming is associated with the Spirit when the angel Gabriel says to Mary: 'The Holy Spirit will come on you, and God's power will rest upon you'.[23] At the baptism of Jesus, Mark reports that John 'saw the heaven opening and the Spirit coming down on him like a dove'.[24] At the inauguration of his ministry, Jesus quoted Isaiah. 'The Spirit of the Lord is upon me.'[25] In the life of Jesus the Spirit bears witness to the new order of creation which is coming into being as the kingdom of God is preached, and the message heard and obeyed. The only unforgivable sin is to deny that the

Holy Spirit is at work as Christ brings this new creation into being.[26]

As the end of his earthly ministry drew near, and it gradually began to dawn upon the disciples that they might be left alone, Jesus increasingly promised them the companionship of the Holy Spirit to lead them into all truth and to guide them in the adventures which lay ahead. The same divine power which had activated his life would be theirs. In St John's gospel where we find the fullest account of the promise of the Spirit, the word used is paraclete, variously translated as advocate, comforter, intercessor, counsellor, helper. The meaning is that of a friend and companion who stands beside you in a court of law, or when undertaking some particularly difficult job, and gives you strength and encouragement by his presence. Jesus who had stood by his disciples during the earthly part of his ministry promises that the Holy Spirit will provide the same personal source of strength and inspiration after his departure. In addition, the gift of the Spirit became particularly associated with witness. The Paraclete will be beside them to interpret the truth about Jesus, and to put the words into their mouths as they embark on their mission to the world.[21]

In a mysterious passage, St John speaks about the promise of the Spirit, and adds that the Spirit had not yet been given because Jesus had not been raised in glory.[28] Perhaps this means that whilst Jesus was with his disciples in the flesh the Spirit did not need to act either as interpreter or guide. Only when Jesus 'was glorified' did the disciples need the indwelling of the Spirit to give them the confidence of his presence and courage and understanding to witness truthfully and boldly.

When was this final promise of Jesus fulfilled that the Holy Spirit would be given to the disciples? The New

Testament records two distinct traditions. In St John the gift of the Spirit is associated directly with the resurrection. It was on the evening of the first Easter day that Jesus appeared to his disciples behind closed doors, and blessed them with the words: 'Receive the Holy Spirit'.[29] But in the Acts of the Apostles the disciples had to wait forty days from Easter to the Ascension, and then another ten days until Pentecost when the Holy Spirit came to them dramatically in the upper room. But in both accounts the two elements of unity ('together in one place'), and mission ('I send you'), were present. And these two elements have always been seen as evidence that the Holy Spirit is guiding the Church.

But it was on the day of Pentecost when the Holy Spirit came in such dramatic form to the assembled disciples that they came to believe that the promise of Jesus had been well and truly fulfilled.[30] The coming of the Spirit was marked by flames of fire, a powerful wind and speaking in tongues. We cannot now precisely know what is meant by the fire and wind, though these have often accompanied psychic manifestations. Speaking with tongues (not foreign languages) was a form of ecstatic speech common in the New Testament Church, and constantly met with in religious revivals ever since. Whatever our assessment of these pentecostal phenomena, they clearly had an important symbolic value in telling the story of the birth of the Church. Fire and wind include a whole host of evocative ideas from cleansing, purifying and melting, to power and driving force. All symbolize the unifying and empowering experience of that notable day. And the speaking in tongues is interpreted as the new language of the gospel which unites men of different races, cultures and traditions, and reverses the divisions of Babel where language became

46

confused because of man's pride.[31]

There has been a revival of interest in the phenomena of the day of Pentecost in the charismatic movement which has influenced church congregations of many denominations and in many parts of the world. They range from emotional and strongly personal forms of worship, including clapping, gesticulating and popular music to ecstatic prophecy, the baptism of the Spirit and speaking in tongues. Some congregations have become enriched and encouraged by this experience, others have become deeply divided because of it. But there is no doubt that the witness of Scripture is that the real sign of activity of the Spirit of God is not so much in the occurrence of bizarre manifestations, but in the congregation which clearly exhibits the fruits of the Spirit. These, say Paul, are love, joy, peace, patience, kindness, goodness, faithfulness, humility and self control.[32] Jesus had promised his disciples that the Holy Spirit would lead them into all truth. During the early years of missionary expansion there were many important decisions to be made both about policy and strategy. They were deeply conscious of their guidance of the Holy Spirit, encouraging them to pursue one course of action, and closing the doors to prevent them from moving in the wrong direction. Millions of Christians throughout the centuries have testified to the same guiding power of the Holy Spirit. The promise of Jesus came marvellously true, and still does. But the promise of the Holy Spirit is not an excuse for mental laziness or for indulgence in superstition or wishful thinking.

The promise of the Spirit was not an invitation to leave reason, intelligence, experience and humour behind. It is a mistake to think we can claim a 'hot line' to God, and that all we have to do is to pick up a receiver to hear the

47

divine voice telling us what we should do next. God treats us as adults and leaves us to use the many faculties he has given us as the means by which to discover his will. The Holy Spirit enables us to use these gifts as the way forward to truth. But always there must be experiment. Guidance must be tried out to see whether it is genuine. Truth is something to be done and not just talked about. The genuineness of our response to the Holy Spirit can only be proved by results. Unity, mission and newness of life are the sure signs of a Spirit filled community. The Spirit of God counteracts human egoism. Where there is reconciliation and unity, there the Spirit is present. Where there is an outgoing concern for other people rather than for self, there the Spirit is at work. Where there is a constant desire to move forward into renewal of life, in art, in family life, in education, in politics, in the nation, in the Church, there are sure indications that the life-giving Spirit is present. It is not for us to make elaborate theories about the Holy Spirit but rather to know how to be conscious of his activity.

We speak of the Spirit in personal terms because we know that his activity is part of that of God who is himself personal. For this reason we cannot speak of the Holy Spirit as 'it'. And we speak of the Holy Spirit in a separate way from the way we speak of God the Father and of Jesus Christ, because our experience of the Spirit derives from the Father and the Son, and yet is somehow separate. If that is puzzling, it need not worry you. In the past it seemed a matter of life and death to speak of the Holy Spirit as the third person of the Trinity, and because there were arguments about this, the Church was split right down the middle. The breach is not yet healed. But for many people these niceties of theological discussion do not matter very much. And they are right.

It is not theology that matters. It is experience. Let the theologians do their best to translate the experience into some kind of logical and intelligible pattern. This is an important and fascinating task, and there are some people whose professional job it is to do it. But do not let ourselves be deluded into thinking that talk about the experience of God is more important than the experience itself. That is a false track. Yet theological questions cannot be avoided. The experience which Christians came to have of God the Father creator, of Jesus Christ, and of the indwelling of the Holy Spirit inevitably led them to ask questions about the nature of God. The word 'trinity' does not appear in the Bible, but the germ of the idea which came to be developed in Christian theology and was incorporated in the creeds was certainly there.

Matthews's gospel finishes with the command of Jesus:

> 'Go to all peoples everywhere and make them my disciples: baptize them in the name of the Father, the Son and the Holy Spirit.'[33]

It is not possible to define what we mean precisely when we proclaim our faith in God as three in one and one in three. Symbols such as the clover leaf or the triangle have been used, though they are not of much help. To speak of God as three 'persons' is also misleading if it gives us a slightly ludicrous picture of the Godhead as a sort of committee of three! Yet within these pictures and words whose meaning we can scarcely begin to grasp lies the concept of God not as solitude but as community. When, in the Genesis story, the Lord sees Adam sitting in isolation in the empty world, he says 'It is not good for the man to be alone,'[34] and creates Eve to be his companion. Man needs to belong. The worst of all punishments is solitary confinement because man only finds his significance and his sanity in the give and take of communal relationships. In marriage, in parenthood, in family life, in school, at work, in neighbourhood, in play, in city and nation and world, man yearns to find a place where he can belong. If he fails to belong he becomes diseased and disorientated. Only as he learns to give and take in the evolving pattern of relationships can he discover his real humanity. And when those relationships are creative and fulfilling they can be given the name of love. God is love, and because he is love he made the world of men and women to grow into relationship with him and to be the recipients of his care. This is so because he is himself love, a community of relationship in perfection, of which all our human relationships are only the palest reflections. We are called in all our dealings one with another to be like him. As we seek to create our own relationships for the good of each individual and the benefit of all, we are slowly discovering what it means to be made in the image of the one who is Father, Son and Holy Spirit, one God, but community in perfect harmony. Here we grope with words and hardly know what we are meaning to say. Yet hidden here is the clue to our deepest experiences and longings.

And because the life of God himself is lived out in relationships, we are called to proclaim the good news not just as isolated individuals but in the community which he himself has called into being through Jesus Christ and in the power of the Spirit. That community is the Church. Its most characteristic activity is worship.

FOR FURTHER THOUGHT AND DISCUSSION ON BELIEF

1. Read Isaiah 40. 21-31,

Psalm 104,
Job 38. 1-42.6.

What value have these passages for the modern reader?
What do they tell you about God, and about yourself?

2. Read 1 Corinthians 1. 18-30.

Why does faith in Jesus Christ still seem to so many to be foolishness?
How can you convince other people that Jesus Christ really is 'the power of God and the wisdom of God'?

3. Read Romans 3. 23-26,
2 Corinthians 5. 21.

What do we really mean when we say 'Jesus saves'? The Bible uses such words as justification, ransom, salvation, redemption, atonement (see pp. 38-40). Which of these words do you find most helpful in talking of the saving power of Jesus Christ?

4. Read John. 14-16.

In what ways are people conscious of the guidance of the Holy Spirit today? How can the genuineness of that guidance be put to the test?
How do you seek for God's guidance in your own life, and how do you recognize that guidance when it comes?

For your prayers:
God the creator

Almighty God
you have created the heaven and the earth

51

and made man in your own image.
Teach us to discern your hand in all your works,
and to serve you
   with reverence and thanksgiving;
through Jesus Christ, our Lord,
who with you and the Holy Spirit
   reigns supreme over all things
now and for ever.

(*ASB*)

Jesus Christ

Thanks be to you, my Lord Jesus Christ,
For all the benefits that you have given me,
For all the pains and insults you have borne for me.
O most merciful Redeemer, Friend and Brother,
May I see you more clearly,
      love you more dearly,
      and follow you more nearly
Day by day.

(*St Richard of Chichester*)

Holy Spirit

O God, empty me of self
   and fill me with your Holy Spirit,
that I may bring forth abundantly
   the fruit of love, joy and peace,
and glorify you day by day
   in a life renewed in the beauty of holiness;
through Jesus Christ our Lord.

(*Frank Colquhoun*)

4. WORSHIP

Jesus and prayer

In the previous chapter we discussed the undertakings you will make at your Confirmation to accept the Christian teaching about God as Father, Son and Holy Spirit. But you will not only say that you believe in God. You will also promise to trust in him. Trust in God is expressed in two ways: in the practice of prayer and in a life of service. As we shall see, prayer and action are closely linked together in the life of those who try to be faithful disciples of Christ and loyal members of his Church.

We believe that God has made himself known to us. Our first response to his self-revelation is prayer. We must speak with him because he has spoken to us first. Prayer is the continuation of a conversation which he has initiated. We often talk of religion as man's search for God, and it often seems like that. But in reality the religious experience is our reply to God's search for us. There is a profound significance put into the mouth of the Lord God as he walked in the garden of Eden in search of sinful Adam. 'The Lord God called to the man and said to him, "Where are you?"'[35] The Psalmist echoed the same theme. Although we can (and do) run away from God, he is always catching up with us.

'O Lord, you have searched me out and known me:

You know when I sit and when I stand
You comprehend my thoughts long before.'[36]

In his spiritual notebook,[37] Cardinal Basil Hume has a section called 'God the Pilgrim — God in search of us'. He writes that if anyone is feeling depressed or downcast or tempted to give up the practice of his faith, he should find some quiet place and read the fifteenth chapter of St Luke's Gospel slowly and prayerfully. This chapter begins with a description of the compassionate ministry of Jesus amongst the sort of people with whom the pious would have no dealings. The Pharisees and the ecclesiastical lawyers grumble that 'this fellow welcomes sinners and eats with them'. In answer Jesus tells three graphic stories. The first is about a shepherd who, losing one of his hundred sheep, leaves the flock to graze in the meadow while he goes into the wild countryside to look for it. The second is about a woman who has mislaid a silver coin (possibly a valuable ornament in her head-dress). She searches and sweeps every corner of her house until at last she finds it. The third story is the parable of the prodigal son who loses himself in reckless spendthrift living in a distant country. Drawn by desperation, he makes his shamefaced way back home only to find his father had already come out to look for him 'while he was still a long way off'. Each of these stories, the search for the lost sheep, the lost coin and the lost son end in great rejoicing, thought the story of the prodigal son, has a sting in the tail. The jealousy of the elder brother was an obvious criticism of the scribes and Pharisees who envied the self-giving love of Jesus in search of those who were lost. You will certainly feel that your decision to be confirmed is a sure sign that God has found you and rejoices that you are coming into the fold of Christ's Church.

These stories also tell us about prayer which is our response to the God who is always searching for us, even when we 'are a great way off'. How do we pray? What are the essential ingredients of the prayer life of the Christian. There is strong evidence that Jesus withdrew at regular intervals from the business of his everyday ministry to spend times of quiet in prayer and meditation. The more busy he was, the more he saw this withdrawal to be essential. He did not pray when he had time for it. He *made* time for it. 'Great crowds gathered to hear him and to be cured of their ailments. And from time to time he would withdraw to lonely places for prayer.'[38] He encouraged his disciples to do the same. 'Come with me, by yourselves, to some lonely place where you can rest quietly (for they had no leisure even to eat, so many were coming and going).'[39] We find also that Jesus always prayed when there were big decisions to be made. Before choosing the twelve apostles he went out into the hills to pray and spent all night there.[40] Before facing the final trial and crucifixion, he distanced himself a little way from his followers in the garden of Gethsemane and prayed that the approaching agony might be taken away from him.[41] The whole life of Jesus was an act of prayer because he was in constant communion with his Father. Yet he made specific times for prayer, including regular attendance at public worship as well as at times of crisis, decision making and pressure of work. As you plan your own pattern of prayer, you should take his example seriously.

The Lord's prayer

But we do not only have his example. We have his teaching. It was customary for Jewish religious teachers to provide a prayer for their followers to say. Jesus did more than that. He not only gave his disciples (and us) a prayer to use daily. He also gave a blueprint upon which all Christian prayer should be based. Matthew[42] tells us that Jesus gave the Lord's prayer to his followers in the course of that great body of teaching we call the sermon on the mount, and it comes within the context of some general teaching about prayer. He told them that they must not use prayer as an excuse for showing off in public. Prayer is likely to be more genuine if offered in the privacy of your own room. Nor should you imagine that the more words you gabble the more likely you are to be heard. As an example of the right kind of praying, he gave the Lord's prayer which is less than a hundred words in length, with every phrase packed with inexhaustable depths of meaning.

Take special note of the sequence of ideas in this great prayer. It begins with a focus on God and his glory, praying that his name may be kept holy, his will may be done, and his kingdom may come. It is only half way through that we are allowed to think of ourselves. Prayer is the act by which we put ourselves consciously into God's hands. It is not a means of grabbing privileges for ourselves. Only as we learn to put God first in our devotional life will we become fit to be instruments of his purpose, and so discover our deepest happiness. We have become accustomed to saying the Lord's prayer quickly and often, without pausing to think what it is we are really saying. We need often to explore the deeper meaning of each of its clauses for we can never exhaust the wisdom and encouragement to be derived from them.

Our Father in heaven. We address the Father as *our* and not *my*. There is no such thing as private prayer, only prayer said in private. Even in the quietness of your own room your prayers are offered within the fellowship of the whole Church of Jesus Christ all over the world. Those who have suffered the penalty of solitary confinement have kept themselves sane in the knowledge that when they prayed the cell became peopled with the communion of saints. We are never alone when we pray. We always enter into the presence of God in the company of his family. Jesus and his disciples were brought up in the religious tradition of the Old Testament and would have been familiar with the description of God as Father. But Jesus gave this idea an entirely new meaning. He used the word *'Abba'* which was the term of endearment with which a child addressed his father within the intimacy of the family circle. It is the equivalent of our word 'daddy'. Jesus used it in the Lord's prayer and also on his knees in Gethsemane. Paul, who in his strict Jewish days would never have spoken of God with such familiarity, on two occasions used this word in his epistles. 'To prove that you are sons, God has sent into our hearts the Spirit of his Son, crying Abba! Father! You are therefore no longer a slave but a son.'[43] Whenever we say Our Father we must thrill that we are able to address almighty God 'in heaven' with such intimate language.

Hallowed be your name. In the Bible a man's name is not just a convenient label given for the purpose of identification. It signifies the essential character of the person so named. Football crowds chant the names of their heroes almost as if they were incantations. Political demonstrators march carrying aloft banners with the names of their chosen leaders. The Psalmist puts his faith in the name of God because he can be trusted:

'Some boast of chariots and some of horses,
but our boast is the name of the Lord our God.'[44]

Paul wrote that God bestowed on Jesus, 'the name

above all names, that at the name of Jesus every knee should bow'.[45] The third commandment said that 'you must not make wrong use of the name of the Lord your God'. The petition in the Lord's prayer turns this negative command into a positive assertion. 'Hallowed be your name' is both a statement of fact (God's name *is* holy) and a prayer that it should always be held in reverence and kept holy. The way we speak about God is a reflection of our attitude towards him. There is a place for humour and fun in our religion, even when we are talking about God. But there is no place for flippancy or coarseness. We should not use any of the names we have for God in a casual or slipshod fashion, as in so much general conversation and on much television. John Newton, the eighteenth century bishop and hymn writer, caught the appropriate mood perfectly when he sang about the sweetness of the name of Jesus.

Dear Name! The rock on which I build,
My shield and hiding place,
My never failing treasury filled
With boundless stores of grace.

We can hallow God's name when we call out an exultant, Thank God! at the experience of falling in love, at the birth of a child, or when an examination is safely passed. Paul urges the people of Thessalonica to be always joyful; pray continually; give thanks whatever happens,[46] for spontaneous thanksgiving to God is a sure way of hallowing his name. So also when we cry, O God!, driven by anguish, panic, disappointment, failure or fear. We can also do honour to God's name in silent adoration, as two lovers may walk hand in hand in silence, their love for each other too deep for words.

My God, how wonderful thou art,
Thy majesty how bright,

How beautiful thy mercy-seat
In depths of burning light!

It is a pity that the great ascription at the conclusion of the letter of Jude which is often spoken at the end of the sermon in Anglican pulpits, should be seen as a sign to the organist to switch on the air pump and for the people in the pews to search for their collection money. It is one of the great Bible outbursts in which the name of God is hallowed.

'To the only God, our Saviour, be glory and majesty, might and authority, through Jesus Christ our Lord, before all time, now, and for evermore.'[47]

Because we worship God as Father and holy, the other clauses in the Lord's prayer follow logically. The coming of his rule on earth is our desire. The doing of his will is our greatest good. And we can come to him in confidence, on behalf of ourselves and of others for bread, for forgiveness, and for guidance.

Your kingdom come. The kingdom of God is the central theme of the teaching of Jesus. It comes at the centre point of the Lord's prayer. The kingdom, as Jesus proclaimed it, is not a geographical location as we might talk about the United Kingdom. It describes what happens when God's purpose for his creation is fully accomplished. Imagine what the world would be like if everybody were perfectly obedient to God's will all the time. This will only come about at the end of time when history has been consummated. Yet Jesus spoke of the signs of the kingdom as being already visible on earth. In his sermon in the Nazareth synagogue he quoted the prophecy of Isaiah proclaiming the announcement of good news to the poor, release for prisoners, recovery of sight for the blind and freedom for the broken victims.

He declared 'Today in your very hearing this text has come true'.[48] When John the Baptist, now in prison, sent messengers to Jesus to find out whether he really was the 'one who was to come', Jesus replied with a demonstration of practical action. 'There and then he cured many sufferers from diseases, plagues and evil spirits; and on many blind people he bestowed sight.'[49] Always in the New Testament talk of the kingdom of God poses a tension between present and future. 'My kingdom is not of this world' said Jesus, and he spoke of an increase in wars and rumours of wars with distress of nations until the end of time.[50] The kingdom is a gift of God which we cannot bring about by our own scheming and blueprints. That is why we have to pray for its coming. No political or economic programme of our own designing will bring it about. Yet we long for a fulfilment of the prayer that the kingdom will come on earth as it is in heaven. We long for a society of equality, justice and truth when God's will is seen to be done amongst men. At this point we have to remember that as far as we are concerned, the kingdom of God begins with us. Our prayer has always to be 'Your kingdom come, starting with me'. As we offer this petition in the Lord's prayer the question it raises for us is, 'How much am I prepared to accept God's rule in my life?' We have to recall the answer that Jesus gave to the Pharisees when they asked him when the kingdom of God would come. His answer was direct, 'There will be no saying, "Look here it is" or "There it is", for in fact the kingdom of God is among you'.[51] Again and again the parables elaborate this theme. The coming of the kingdom is like a tiny mustard seed which grows into a great tree, or like the influence of a spoonful of yeast mixed with half a hundredweight of flour. Great things spring from small beginnings. But this can only happen if in our prayers and in our actions we learn how to work together with God to bring his kingdom on earth. This must be given the same priority as a merchant gives in his search for the most precious gems. Where you live and work, you are one of God's agents in his plan for realizing the kingdom in the world.[52]

But how can we tell that we are praying for the right things when we say 'Your kingdom come'? The next clause in the Lord's prayer provides the answer.

Your will be done on earth as in heaven. Immediately we say this petition we are reminded of one of the most moving moments in the life of Jesus. 'Father, if it be thy will, take this cup from me. Yet not my will, but thine be done.' The test of the rightness of our intentions as we pray must be to discover whether what we are saying is in accordance with God's will. This we learn from looking carefully at the example and teaching of Jesus, who said that his meat and drink was to do the will of the Father who sent him.[53] That is why we dare to put our prayers to the test by offering them 'through Jesus Christ our Lord'. This is no empty formula, though it is often made to sound as such. It expresses our will to join our prayers with the perfect prayer of Jesus 'who lives to make intercession for us'.[54] We make our petitions through Jesus Christ, because there can be no validity in our prayers unless we learn to pray with his mind. We know that if we 'have the mind of Christ' our prayers will not go unheard.

But the phrase 'your will be done', sometimes receives shabby treatment when it is used to suggest the passive and reluctant acceptance of the inevitable. It indicates a feeling of resignation, even of resentment. When in spite of our prayers someone we love dies following a tragic accident, or a fatal illness, we are tempted to sigh 'God's will be done'. But often our better instincts tell us that the accident or the illness is not God's will, and we want to cry out: 'It isn't fair'. That, in itself, is a valid form of prayer. For prayer is not always answered in the way we want. Things sometimes happen in a way that God does not want either. At such moments we are faced with a mystery which we cannot solve. But this does not mean we should cease praying:

> Blind unbelief is sure to err,
> And scan his work in vain; ▪
> God is his own interpreter,
> And he will make it plain.[55]

We can still pray 'your will be done', confident that even when life is most difficult and bewildering, he who rose from this prayer and had to face the cross can be with us in our anguish, bringing good out of the evil. We pray in companionship with him, knowing that beyond Calvary lies resurrection.

Give us today our daily bread. Many people think of prayer as primarily to do with asking God for things. But it is only half way through the Lord's prayer that we request something for ourselves. And our demand is modest. We ask for bread, for what is necessary to keep us healthy and fit for our daily work and responsibilities. We are not asking for luxuries. And though most of us can be certain that bread will be available for us tomorrow whether we pray for it or not, the Lord's prayer comes as a daily reminder that we are totally dependent upon God for all we have and for life itself.

The Greek word usually translated 'daily' is a rare one. It means 'enough for the coming day'. It is a reminder that we should not be concerned with the hoarding of material possessions right into the future. There is a strong tradition in Christian spirituality that we should learn to live one day at a time. As Cardinal Newman expressed it: 'I do not ask to see the distant scene, one step enough for me.' This is not an easy philosophy at a time when there is so much emphasis on prudent planning for the future through savings schemes, insurance policies, building societies and the like. Nor is it appropriate for Christians living in comfortable circumstances to tell the poor of the world (or of their own community) that they should learn to sit lightly to this world's goods. Yet we cannot ignore the insistent teaching of Jesus against the laying up of treasures upon earth, and putting our hearts on them. The Lord's prayer, with its request for enough bread for the day is a constant reminder of that passage in the sermon on the mount when Jesus said: 'Do not ask anxiously, "What are we to eat, what are we to drink? What shall we wear? ..." Do not be anxious about tomorrow, tomorrow will look after itself'.[56] We each have the difficult task of working out what these uncomfortable words have to say to us about our own style of living.

Nor is the prayer focused only on my needs. We pray to *our* Father to supply the needs of all of us. It is easy to fall into the trap of making our prayers self-centred. Spontaneous petitions at prayer meetings often suggest a selfish attitude of 'please God look after me'. When we pray to God to give us our daily bread, we are bringing to him our concern for the hungry, illiterate, homeless, diseased and persecuted people of the world as well as those within our more immediate circle who are sick, unemployed or in any kind of trouble.

But why is it necessary to bring these things to God in prayer? A well known prayer speaks of God as 'knowing our necessities before we ask, and our ignorance in asking'. Jesus spoke of the boy asking his father for food:

'If you, bad as you are, know how to give your children what is good for them, how much more will your heavenly Father give good things to those who ask him'. Yet he taught his disciples to ask so that they might receive, and illustrated the point by telling two vivid stories. One tells about a man who went to wake up his neighbour, even though it was past midnight, and his family were all in bed, because a guest had unexpectedly arrived and he had no bread to give him.[57] The other was the story of a widow who persisted so vigorously in the court of a thoughtless judge that she finally, after much pestering, obtained the justice she sought.[58]

Of course God gives his good gifts to those who do not or cannot ask him. His generosity does not depend on our requests. Nor do we pray as if God did not understand our needs much better than we do. We pray in order to express our dependence on him, to deepen our understanding of his purpose for us, and to widen the horizons of our compassion. The Lord's prayer relates our temporal needs to God's eternal plan. Answer to prayer will be most evident in our growing awareness of God's will for us and his world, and in our renewed determination to go into action for the sake of the kingdom of God. Bishop Ramsey has written: 'If prayer and life are interwoven then the right question may not be "What good does prayer do" but "What good does the praying Christian do".'[59]

It is certainly not our job to bombard God with our requests in the hope that we can cajole him into changing his mind. An evening prayer rightly speaks of God's changelessness. But this does not mean that it is a waste of time praying for other people or for ourselves. Prayer helps us to discern the way that God wants to meet our needs. He may do this by apparently granting our request or by rejecting it. The answer may come provided we make our own contribution towards bringing it about. A prayer which seems to be unanswered and unheard may be seen, by hindsight many months later, to have been answered positively in a quite different way from what we expected. There is plenty of evidence to show that other people can be helped immensely by our prayers, even if at the time they did not know that we were praying for them. Paul in prison rejoiced in his letter to the church members in Philippi, 'knowing well that the issue of it all will be my deliverance, because you are praying for me'.[60]

Does God interfere with the laws of nature in answer to the prayers we offer for ourselves and other people? Does he send rain in time of drought, or change the medical course of events miraculously when someone is dying of cancer? There is certainly some evidence (not only among Christians) of answers to prayer which seem to reverse the normal course of cause and effect as we understand them at present. But we have to be clear that God has created an ordered, though sometimes mysterious, universe, with its own physical laws. If those laws were always changing, life as we know it would quickly become impossible. God has laid down a normal pattern in creation, and we must not expect him to tamper with it for our own personal convenience. The whole world is in God's hands and he can be seen to be as much at work in the ordinary course of nature which can be analysed in scientific terms, as in events which some people might consider to be miraculous.

The real answer to prayer comes in the courage to meet adversity, in the transformation of evil into good, the renewal of faith, and the action which is the sign of continuing trust.

Forgive our sins as we forgive those who sin against us. There can be no true prayer which does not include penitence because no one can claim to be without sin. 'All alike have sinned and are deprived of the divine splendour.'[61] As the writer of the first letter of John stated bluntly, anyone who claims to be sinless deceives himself.[62] The Prayer Book services of Morning and Evening Prayer, and of Holy Communion include prayers asking for forgiveness. Penitence must also have a part in our personal devotions. We know that we can be forgiven, for Jesus demonstrated by word and deed the unconditional forgiveness of God. Even when he was being nailed to the cross, he prayed to God to forgive his executioners. Central to the good news of our faith is the assurance that we do not have to earn forgiveness. It is God's free gift. 'Christ died for us while we were yet sinners.'[63]

But even gifts which are freely offered have to be accepted if they are not to fall to the ground. This was the sin of the Pharisees. They refused to accept the gift offered to them. Hans Küng has written, that Jesus shook the very foundations of religion because in his teaching traitors, swindlers and adulterers were put in the right as against the devout and righteous.[64] The forgiveness of God is offered without any conditions. But the Lord's prayer teaches us that the test of our willingness to receive this gift is seen in our readiness to forgive those who have wronged us. We cannot be forgiven unless we are forgiving. The parable of the unmerciful servant graphically illustrates this teaching.[65] The Lord's prayer reminds us of it daily.

Lead us not into temptation, but deliver us from evil. Many people have found great difficulty in this petition which asks that God will not lead us into temptation. Did

Jesus mean to suggest that God might actually want to put temptation deliberately in our path? If you look at this part of the prayer in a modern translation of the Bible, you will find a solution to this problem. In the New English Bible the prayer is that we should 'not be brought to the test'. The Good News Bible puts it even more clearly. 'Do not bring us to hard testing.' Another version speaks of being delivered from 'the time of trial'. These translations, reflected in many of the revised prayer books in use in the Anglican Communion, help us to understand what Jesus intended when he taught his disciples to use these words when they prayed. God does not go out of his way to lead us astray, but if you try to be faithful to the leadership of Christ, you will often find your faith and your loyalty severely put to the test. You know what it is to compromise, to deny, or to keep silent when you should have spoken out. You know the struggle to maintain honesty, truthfulness, purity, humility and love in the face of all the pressures which come from both inside and outside ourselves. This is the natural lot of the Christian and we must not put the blame on God. 'No one under trial or temptation should say: "I am being tempted by God"; for God is untouched by evil and does not tempt anyone.'[66] But our prayers may legitimately be made to God that we should not be tested beyond our endurance. God knows our limits better than we do. Jesus prayed that Peter's faith might not fail and 'When you have come to yourself, you must lend strength to your brothers'.[67] Paul describes the sharp physical pain which must have caused him severe disability and which he described as 'Satan's messenger to bruise me'. Three times he prayed for relief. The answer came to him 'My grace is all you need: power comes to its full strength in weakness'.[68]

Temptation is not sin unless it is courted deliberately. The writer to the Hebrews says 'Jesus, because of his likeness to us, has been tested every way, only without sin'.[69] God can deliver us from trial because he delivered Jesus and led him to victory. Paul's words to the Corinthians can provide you with a firm foundation and confidence as you set out on the perilous path of the Christian life:

> 'So far you have faced no trial beyond what man can bear. God keeps faith, and he will not allow you to be tested above your powers, but when the test comes he will at the same time provide a way out, by enabling you to sustain it.'[70]

So the Lord's prayer provides a synopsis for the prayer life of the Christian:

> God's holiness, kingdom and will;
> our needs and those of other people;
> reconciliation with God and others;
> power to lead the Christian life.

Adoration, praise, thanksgiving, intercession, petition, penitence and dedication are all there in the prayer that Jesus taught us to use. How you make this part of your life as a committed Christian will be discussed in the final section of this book.

The Eucharist

From earliest times Christians have met together week by week on Sunday for common prayer, and particularly for the celebration of the Eucharist. Regular meetings for public worship remain the central part of the disciplined life of a committed Christian. By your Confirmation you undertake to share with your fellow Christians in the

68

place where you live in the regular offering of worship within the fellowship of the world-wide Church.

Recent years have seen considerable changes in the pattern of Sunday worship. Until a short time ago the staple diet in most Anglican churches was Morning and Evening Prayer (or Matins and Evensong) with Holy Communion in the early morning (often called 'early service') for the more committed, or again after morning service for the less energetic (sometimes called 'staying behind'). Increasingly Holy Communion has become the main service of the day, with Evensong (with much diminished attendance in most places) in the early evening. In some churches Matins has vanished altogether on a Sunday. This new central emphasis on the Eucharist has been a great gain, though there has been some loss in the importance given to Bible reading and preaching which in the Church of England have been valued features of morning and evening prayer.

It is reckoned that two hundred million people meet for the sacrament of Holy Communion all over the world each week. This almost certainly makes it the most numerous regular gathering of human beings meeting around a common theme and for a common purpose that the modern world knows. If you go to a service of Holy Communion in a little church somewhere with only a handful of communicants present, it is worth remembering this. You are part of a mighty company. The Holy Communion has this supreme position within Christian worship because it is the only service initiated by our Lord himself.

What do we do when we celebrate the Holy Communion? As one of the thanksgiving prayers in the ASB says 'We make with this bread and this cup the memorial of Christ your Son our Lord'. Yet it is more than a memorial meal. It is not the same as an old boys' reunion, to remember with nostalgia the days gone by. It is not like the endless queue in Moscow's Red Square waiting to file past the dead body of Lenin. We do not come to Holy Communion to mourn a death but to celebrate life. As the bread and the wine are blessed, we make the great affirmation of the mystery of our faith.

Christ has died.

Christ is risen.

Christ will come again.

In this celebration past (has), present (is) and future (will) are held together in a single moment. And because we believe that the Christ who came once upon a time, and who will come again at the end of time is actually with us now in this sacrament, we dare to say (as he taught us) that the bread is his body and the wine is his blood. The bread and wine are not physically turned into flesh and blood. The priest is not there to perform magic. The Roman Catholic Church has a doctrine of transubstantiation in which it teaches (with varied interpretations) that Jesus Christ is physically, in some sense, there on the altar. Anglicans are not committed to such a view, or to any particular theory about 'what happens'. Different Anglicans have different explanations to account for this experience of the presence of Christ in the Eucharist. It is not the theories but the experience itself that matters. The Eucharist gives the assurance that we meet with our Lord as we take the bread and the wine, that through this sacrament we know that we can 'evermore dwell in him and he in us', and that we can live our lives with the encouraging good news that the Lord is here and his Spirit is with us. Most Anglicans are content with the reply alleged to have been given by Queen Elizabeth I when asked her views about Christ's presence in the sacrament.

> 'Twas God the Word that spake it
> He took the bread and break it
> And what the Word did make it
> That I believe and take it.

People are sometimes puzzled by the different names that are given to this service. Some are even frightened and see something sinister in the names that other people use. But there is good sense in all of them. Holy Communion indicates the fellowship we have with Christ and one another. Mass comes from the same word as mission. We are sent out from this sacrament to do God's work in the world. The Lord's Supper is a reminder that this is a family meal at which Jesus is our host. Eucharist, which simply means thanksgiving, is probably the oldest name for the service, and has lately come into much more common use.

Not only in churches of different denominations but also within the family of Anglican churches the Eucharist is celebrated in many different ways. Sometimes it is accompanied by much ceremonial and ritual with candles, processions, elaborate vestments, incense with many clergy and acolytes taking part. Sometimes there is no music at all. The Eucharist can be celebrated in a great cathedral, in the sitting room of a house, in a hospital ward, in a school room, in the open air. We may have our own personal preference for the way the service is done and even be suspicious of the unfamiliar ('Thank God we do not do it like this in our church'). This is a poor attitude to adopt. We have so much to learn from being present when the Eucharist is celebrated in another denomination or tradition, or in another country in an unfamiliar language.

But whatever church you attend, the pattern of the

Eucharist is likely to be very much the same. This outline is based on the Rite A Order in the ASB but you will find the same themes appearing in other versions which may be used in your local church.

Preparation. After a greeting and a prayer asking for the inspiration and cleansing of the Holy Spirit, the act of penitence follows. The commandments or the summary of the Law remind us of our Christian duty to love God with heart, soul, mind and strength, and our neighbours as ourselves. Because we have failed to do this, and yet continue to have faith in God's loving forgiveness, we make an act of confession for past sins and resolve that in the future we may serve God in newness of life. The absolution declares God's promise of mercy and strength for making a fresh start. Unless we truly repent of our sins and are in love and charity with our neighbours, we dare not presume to draw near to receive the sacrament.

After the absolution we sing (or say) the ancient hymn Gloria in Excelsis, originally written in Latin, in which we express both the praise which is due to God, and our continual need of his mercy.

Ministry of the Word. The service of Holy Communion falls into two main sections, Word and Sacrament. We first hear the good news of Jesus Christ, and then, in obedience to him, do the sacrament as he has commanded us. The Word consists of readings from the Old Testament, the Epistle and the Gospel, declaring the mighty works of God in history, in the Church, and above all in Jesus Christ. The readings are prefaced by a special prayer for each Sunday called the collect, because it collects up the thoughts appropriate for that day. The ministry of the word concludes with a sermon, usually elaborating the theme of the readings, and everyone joins in with the Nicene creed, dating from the year 325, as a summary of the beliefs which bring us together in worship. Sometimes the act of penitence follows rather than precedes the ministry of the Word. We have heard of God's great love for us, and we are bound to acknowledge the feebleness of our response.

Prayers. Before proceeding to the celebration of the sacrament, we remember before God not only our own needs but those of the whole world. The intercessions can take a number of forms of greater or lesser formality. The general pattern is likely to include prayers for the work of the Church, both locally and throughout the world, for our country and its leaders, for justice and peace in every land, for families, friends and neighbours and for all who suffer. Because the sacrament is celebrated within the context of the whole Church, past, present and future, the prayers conclude with a thankful remembrance of all who have died in the Christian faith.

The Peace. Having put our celebration within the setting of the whole Church in the world, we now greet one another in the congregation with the sign of peace. This is a very ancient and worthwhile custom dating from at least the second century, and probably going right back to the time of the apostles. Despite its antiquity, this custom has only lately been reintroduced into Anglican worship. Some congregations are still reluctant to take part in it even though today the normal greeting is a hand clasp and not, as in former times, a kiss!

The Offertory. This is an important part of our preparation for the sacrament. Bread and wine, which represent both the bounty of God and the work of human hands are offered for use in the celebration. In many churches representatives of the congregation bring the bread and wine from the body of the church to the altar, together with the money collected from the people. All things come from God, and of his own do we give him.

The Thanksgiving. The prayer of thanksgiving and consecration begins with the proclamation 'Lift up your hearts'. The Sursum Corda was already in use in the third century, and together with the Gloria in Excelsis and the Agnus Dei has been in constant use in the Eucharist from the earliest times. Jesus once said that a wise scribe is he who takes out of his treasure chest things both old and new. It is fitting that whenever we worship God we should not only use prayers and hymns written in our own times, but also use words which recall our roots right from the beginning of the Christian story.

The ancient prayers and praises at the heart of the Eucharist are used in almost all churches, as is the repetition of the story of the last supper firmly based on the evidence of Scripture. The biblical record is recited between a proclamation of God's great work in creation, in history and in the Church, and a prayer that we, by sharing in this sacrament, may be renewed by God's Spirit, inspired by his love, and united in Christ's body. This longing for unity is then expressed as we say the Lord's prayer together. Then the bread is broken, and the Agnus Dei (O Lamb of God) said or sung. In the Anglican tradition the bread and wine are usually received kneeling. This is an intensely personal moment. The priest invites the people to draw near with faith to receive the body and blood of our Lord Jesus Christ. The Eucharist is the great corporate act of the Church, yet the moment of receiving at the communion rail is one of close personal encounter with the Lord. The body given for *you*. The blood shed for *you*.

Conclusion. After all have received communion, the service ends quickly in most modern rites. There is, in Rite A, a post communion prayer of great beauty, dedicating the worshipper to lead his Christian life more worthily in the days ahead.

'May we who share Christ's body live his risen life; we who drink his cup, bring life to others; we whom the Spirit lights, give light to the world.'

And after a final blessing, we are exhorted to go in peace to love and serve the Lord.

FOR FURTHER THOUGHT AND DISCUSSION ON WORSHIP

1. Read Luke 15.

In what ways (if any) are you aware of yourself being 'lost'?
In what ways do you think God is searching for you?

2. Read Luke 5.16,
   Mark 6. 31,
   Luke 6. 12,
   Luke 22. 42.

What can we learn today from these glimpses of Jesus at prayer?

3. Read Matthew 6. 1-18,
   Matthew 7. 7-12,
   Luke 11. 5-13,
   Luke 18. 1-8.

What practical things do these passages tell us about our approach to the life of prayer?

For your prayers:

Almighty God, the fountain of all wisdom, you

know our needs before we ask, and our ignorance in asking; have compassion on our weakness, and give us those things which for our unworthiness we dare not, and for our blindness we cannot ask, for the sake of your Son, Jesus Christ, our Lord.

(*ASB*)

5. SERVICE

The call to serve

When on your Confirmation day you make your solemn declaration to turn to Christ, you do not only commit yourself to a life of faith, worship and prayer. Turning to Christ also means turning to your neighbour in love, compassion and service. Ever since New Testament times Christians have argued whether faith or good works should be considered the more important. It is a sterile argument. The particular genius of Christianity is that a person's faith in God and his service to his neighbour are inextricably bound together. To separate the one from the other is to court disaster. Faith in God and the worship which flows from it, divorced from the practical expression of love for our fellow men, easily degenerates into self-seeking pietism. But good works, divorced from a living faith in God as expressed in personal prayer and corporate worship can be a sort of humanism which finally fails to satisfy the needs of the whole person.

The necessity of compassionate action to authenticate the faith which the Christian proclaims with his lips is a major theme in the Epistle of James:

> The kind of religion which is without stain or fault in the sight of God our Father is this: to go to the help of orphans and widows in their distress and

keep oneself untarnished by the world.[71]

Later the writer daringly adds that if faith does not lead to action, it is in itself a lifeless thing. For those who wish to turn to Christ it is of the greatest significance that the invitation to Peter to make a personal act of commitment to Jesus and the experience of the three chosen apostles as they worship the transfigured Lord on the mountain top is immediately followed by the healing of the epileptic boy when, we are told, the eyewitnesses were struck with awe at the majesty of God.

Jesus 'went about doing good'. He inaugurated his ministry with a massive campaign of healing and compassion. The crowds flocked to him in their thousands because they knew that here was someone who cared about their most pressing needs and would do all in his power to help them. When he taught people that God was a loving Father they knew that it was true because he taught not only in words but through practical action. When, during his final days on earth, he was training his disciples to continue his work after he had left them, he washed their feet as a dramatic way of showing that service lay at the heart of the Christian mission.[72]

By your Baptism and Confirmation you make public your readiness to stand up and be counted amongst the disciples of Jesus who called himself a servant. This is a privilege to treasure. But it also brings great responsibilities. Those around you will judge the genuineness of your commitment by what they can see of your attitude towards other people, and especially towards the needy, the despised and the misunderstood in your community. A church which is largely preoccupied with its own domestic life or its own prestige is a poor advertisement for that religion of love which Jesus came to teach. However efficiently a church may be organized and

78

however diligent its members may be in their personal prayers and Bible reading, in their attendance at worship, and in their participation in church activities, if there is not an evident concern for the welfare of those who live in their neighbourhood and in the wider world, this must surely be a sign of failure in basic discipleship.

You should never think of the church you go to as the exclusive property of those who claim to be its members. The Church to which you are now to commit yourself belongs solely to Christ, and he gave it for the sake of the whole world. Some hymns and prayers in popular usage suggest that it is a sort of exclusive club in which to find a refuge from real life, a cosy ark in which the privileged can ride the storm, a bosom in which to hide. But the Church exists primarily for those who do not belong to it. It is not a shelter in which to escape from the realities of day to day existence. It is more like the headquarters of a fire brigade or salvage corps where people are trained and equipment kept in good working order, ready at any moment to respond to need as it arises. You must not think of the Church into which you are committing yourself by Confirmation simply as an organization you have chosen to join. You must see it as a base from which you are summoned to go out to witness to your Lord by effective service in the world. Someone once said that on the day of Pentecost the Holy Spirit came like a rushing mighty wind and blew the disciples out of the Church! The New Testament describes the remarkable missionary expansion of those early days. 'As for those who had been scattered, they went through the country preaching the word.'[73]

The Gospel was preached not only by the words they used but by their dedicated lives of self-sacrificing compassion. Jesus had told his disciples that they were to be like salt and light in the world. Salt gives flavour not by remaining in a lump by itself, but by infiltrating the whole dish in order to bring out its flavour. Light moves at great speed in waves from its source to the surface it is intended to illuminate. Salt and light can only do their job by moving towards the thing that needs flavouring or illuminating.[74] Mission is always a question of movement from the Church out into the world in the name of Christ. A church which is not organized for service as well as for services forfeits the right to call itself a true church of Jesus Christ, however impeccable its orthodoxy and however impressive its worship.

'Doing good'

Some of the practical ways in which you can respond to this aspect of turning to Christ will be outlined in the next chapter. But there is one further idea which you should think about if you are to understand what it means to serve the world in the name of Jesus Christ who himself went about doing good. Nobody could wish for a finer epitaph than that 'he did good'. Yet in recent years the phrase 'doing good' has come into some disrepute. To call someone a 'do-gooder' can even be intended as an insult. It suggests a busy-body who interferes in other people's business, or who tries to manipulate them for his own purposes. Jesus never manipulated people because he took men and women seriously as individuals in their own right, accepting them as they were, and being ready to receive from them as well as to give to them. Because of this respect in which he held the many and varied people he encountered during his earthly ministry, he was able to come very close to them, understanding their real needs. He could bring hope, courage, and healing to their sickness of body, mind and spirit because he understood the deepest levels of their being. This is the give and take of real sympathy.

Christian caring means a readiness to accept from people as well as to give to people. Doing good to others recognizes the good that others can do to us, even those who may appear to be least able to offer anything. People in need do not want to be patronized. They want to be accepted as persons, not as 'cases'. Jesus never patronized people. He always wanted to enter into a receiving as well as a giving relationship with them. Nobody who has cared for those who are mentally or physically handicapped or are in the terminal stages of a severe illness can deny that they have gained as much (perhaps more) from the relationship as they were able to give. It is not only the poor, the handicapped, the disadvantaged, the oppressed who need us. We need them in order to puncture our own false sense of security and well-being, and to help us to face up to our own desperate need for healing, cleansing and assurance. At an international conference on the serving ministry of the Church, a group reported with these questions:

> 'Can we admit that we are all handicapped and all normal. Can we understand how to receive from those we believe to be handicapped? To be without legs, to be deaf, to be old is not less than normal. Our own lack of faith may be a greater handicap. Does our ecclesiasticism separate us from secular people who have spiritual needs, and so we decide what we will give to people before we have listened to them?'

These are uncomfortable questions. Service must be seen to be as much an essential ingredient of real life for ourselves as we hope it may be for those we try to serve. That is why you will have to evaluate very seriously what part service to others should take in your personal list of priorities. It is in serving others that we serve Christ. For many have found by experience that when they have come face to face with those in greatest need, they have come face to face with Jesus.

FOR FURTHER THOUGHT AND DISCUSSION ON SERVICE

1. Read John 13. 1-17.

   What was Jesus trying to teach his disciples by this action at such a critical moment?
   What does it say to us today?

2. Read Luke 10. 25-37.

   Note the four actions of the good neighbour in verses 33-35.
   He saw.
   He went over to him.
   He poured wine and oil into the wounds (first aid).
   He arranged accommodation (long term care).
   Can you translate these four actions into the Christian response to human need today both in the action of the individual who claims to be a follower of Christ, and in the local congregation?

3. Read Matthew 25. 31-46.

   How does this parable describe the needs of those both on the world level and in the local community?
   In what practical ways should the Christian respond

to these needs, and receive the blessing 'Anything you did for them, you did for me'?

For your prayers:

> Almighty Father
>   whose Son has taught us
> that what we do for the least of our brethren
>   we do also for him:
> give us the will to be the servant of others
>   as he was the servant of all,
> who gave his life and died for us
>   yet is alive and reigns with you and the Holy Spirit one God, now and for ever.
>
> (ASB)

6. BEING AN ANGLICAN

You must belong

When the bishop lays his hands upon those who have come to be confirmed, he invites the congregation to join with him in welcoming them into the Lord's family.

'We are members together of the body of Christ;
we are children of the same heavenly Father;
we are inheritors together of the kingdom of God.
We welcome you.'

By Baptism and Confirmation you are not only admitted into the membership of your own local church or even of the Church of England or some other part of the Anglican Communion. You become part of the one, holy, catholic and apostolic Church, the family of God existing all down history and all over the earth. Baptism and Confirmation do not just make you an Anglican. They make you a Christian and a member of the body of Christ. Our ecclesiastical divisions and our own short-sightedness can easily obscure this great fact. But it is a glorious reality, and it should fill you with joy.

But is it necessary to belong to the Church? Why cannot you be a Christian without having to join? Is the Church a necessary part of Christianity? The answer is an emphatic Yes. This is the way God works. From the earliest times God has called men and women into a close relationship with himself and with one another for their own well-being, and for carrying out his purposes in the world. Evidence for this dates far back to the time of Abraham and Moses when God made a covenant with his people and declared 'I will adopt you as my people, and I will become your God'.[75] Jesus called his disciples into a new covenant to be in intimate fellowship with him and with one another so that he could send them out with confidence to proclaim his kingdom. He described that fellowship as being like a vine and it branches.[76] Paul saw Baptism as the way converts were made members of this body to share the work of the new covenant.[77] Peter wrote to his Christian friends, 'You are now the people of God who once were not his people',[78] and through many other vivid word pictures we get of the first Christian communities in the Acts of the Apostles, the emphasis is all the time on belonging.

> 'They met constantly to hear the apostles teach, and to share the common life, to break bread and to pray.'[79]

And in the Holy Communion Service today the priest affirms:

> 'You have sent upon us your holy and life-giving Spirit, and made us a people for your own possession.'

You could use those words to describe your hopes and prayers for your own Confirmation.

If there were no Church, there would be no faith, no Bible, no sacraments. There would be no Christians because only through the work of the Church can there be mission. Membership of the Church is not an optional extra in the life of the Christian. It is essential to it. No wonder the bishop and people will welcome you so warmly into its fellowship.

In our everyday experience people meet together in

clubs and organizations to do three things. They meet to enjoy sharing a common experience as in a stamp collectors', gardeners' or sports club. They meet to learn from one another and encourage one another as in an old people's club, an evening class, a riding school or Alcoholics Anonymous. They meet because they want to promote practical action, as in a political party, a Rotary Club or a civic society. Christians meet in the Church for the same reasons. They meet to share and deepen their experience of Jesus Christ, to learn more about the meaning of discipleship, and to equip themselves for Christian mission and service. To do these things, we need the Church. Equally, for these purposes, the Church needs us. We are called to belong not only for what we can gain from our membership, but for what we can give to others. We join in order to strengthen the faith of others, to help the Church to be more completely the people of God on earth, to be ambassadors for Christ's sake amongst those with whom we live and work. And if you feel like saying, 'Who am I to do these great and difficult things?', remember that we belong to the Church not because we are better than other people, but because Jesus Christ has called us into membership.

Your local church

Belonging to the world-wide Church means linking up with your local church. It is there that you must worship, receive the sacraments, grow in faith, and learn the meaning of Christian fellowship and service. For your local church is your nearest branch of the people of God, and that is where you belong. It is easy to poke fun at the average Anglican congregation by saying (as some do) that it is middle-aged, middle class, and predominantly female. Maybe some are like that. But many church congregations represent a wider cross-section of the community as a whole than you are likely to find in your local political parties, trades union groups or sports associations. It has to be admitted that when they meet together the words these church members say and sing may sound rather more splendid than the deeds and attitudes they actually show. They like singing lustily that no goblin or foul fiend shall daunt their spirit, yet can get remarkably anxious when a new order of service or a new hymn tune is introduced. Claims to be 'Christian soldiers marching as to war' look a little lame when members of the parochial church council reveal a greater interest in looking back to the past than in marching into the future with courage and imagination. Paul's words to the congregation which met in Corinth still ring true:

'Think what sort of people you are, whom God has called. Few of you are men of wisdom, by any human standard; few are powerful or highly born. Yet, to shame the wise, God has chosen what the world counts folly, and to shame what is strong, God has chosen what the world counts weakness. He has chosen things low and contemptible, to overthrow the existing order. And so there is no place for human pride in the presence of God.'[80]

When you join a church you are not becoming a member of a club for the extremely virtuous holy or intelligent. You are joining an ordinary group of men and women whose only claim to be out of the ordinary is that they know God has called them to witness to him together in the place where they live and worship. That is an extraordinary claim!

As a confirmed member it is your duty to make the

best contribution you can to the life of your local church. Each member matters to the whole, for a church is as strong as it weakest link. You must play your part in it loyally and steadfastly, not only for your own benefit, but for the good of everyone. You should be as regular in worship as your circumstances allow. Those who attend spasmodically or when 'they feel like it', weaken the life of the whole congregation. Empty pews are a poor advertisement for those who claim to have turned to Christ. You must be as generous as you can with your time, talents and money. Remember it costs as much to run your church whether you are there or not. Stewardship schemes which encourage regular giving help a church to balance its books even when a succession of bad weather Sundays keep some regular worshippers at home. Even more than your money, your local church wants you with your particular talents and gifts of personality. What have you to place at the disposal of your local church? Writers and artists can help produce a parish magazine or other publicity material. People with typing and secretarial skills are always in demand as are music and drama enthusiasts. Those who are of mechanical bent or good at gardening or decorating can help the church buildings and grounds from looking shabby and neglected. Cooks and caterers (men as well as women) are always needed. So are drivers (with their cars) to bring the elderly and infirm to services and other church events. Those who are good at teaching (not necessarily or even primarily professional teachers) are sure to find a job in the church's educational programme, with adults and young people as well as children. And those who have the gift of leadership and wise decision-making are wanted on parochial church councils, and finance and other committees. In many parishes these jobs are done by a handful of people. By becoming an active member of your church you can help to spread the load. But a word of warning is needed. If some people give too little time to their church, others give too much. You have important commitments to your family, friends, work, and the things in which you are involved outside the church, and these may be of equal or greater importance. Get your priorities straight, and balance conflicting claims sensibly.

As a member of your local church you have a responsibility in taking your share in creating a genuine spirit of love and trust among its members. Feuds, tensions, rival factions can destroy a parish and do great dishonour to God. When it was remarked of the first Christians 'how they loved one another', this was a reflection of what outsiders could actually observe. The phrase is now sometimes sadly used in mockery. As you take your part in the life of the local congregation there are some serious questions you have to ask. Is there a failure of mutual trust and confidence between clergy and laity so that they are unable to 'speak the truth in love' to one another for the good of all? Are the church officials more intent on grabbing power and prestige than seeing themselves as the servants of the whole congregation? Is there a continuation of the old fashioned sexual stereotyping which means that all the most responsible jobs are given to men and that women are left to do the 'housewifely things' such as catering or stallholding at bazaars, with little say in making decisions which matter? Do the members of the choir not only enter the church on Sundays by a special door, but also feel themselves to be separated from the main life of the church, with little sense of their part in its total mission and ministry? Are young and old kept in separate compartments, with little mutual understanding or co-operation? Are the wealthier or 'higher class' parishioners shown more honour and deference by clergy and people than those who are lowlier? In multiracial areas, does the congregation reflect the ethnic pattern of the secular community, and also demonstrate that the colour of a man's skin can make no difference to the place he holds in the Christian family? Do the various parochial organizations, for men, for women, for young people, help to forward the unity of the parish, or do they break it up into segments, with a primary loyalty to the particular organization rather than to the whole Christian community? In parishes which have experienced some kind of charismatic renewal, has this helped towards the unity of the people of God in that place, or has it created fresh divisions between those who feel themselves to be the in-group, and the rest? Does the pattern of worship help towards the total unity of the people of the parish, or do a variety of services at different times and of various kinds serve to provide an *à la carte* menu of worship in which each group chooses its own particular fare according to its own taste and convenience without experiencing the sense of the whole Christian community at prayer together in this place?

As you ask yourself such questions you must not let yourself feel superior to your fellow church members, or allow insensitive criticism to cause even more division or misunderstanding. But as you begin to take your full part in the life of your local church, these are the kind of issues you should take seriously in the light of the blessing which Jesus promised to the peacemakers. The good news of Jesus the reconciler will not be evident in a parish at sixes and sevens with itself.

But your responsibility cannot be confined to what happens in the church and parochial buildings.

Throughout the centuries the parishes of the Church of England have tried to meet the needs of the secular community by the provision of charitable trusts, by schemes for the young, the sick and the old, by education, by social fellowship and leisure time entertainment. In theory the Church of England priest has a responsibility for the spiritual well-being of all who reside in his parish and who have not joined another religious body. Most urban parishes today are too densely populated to allow the priest to fulfil his pastoral role to everyone who lives within his boundaries. In the country the parish priest may have half a dozen scattered villages under his care. Shortage of finance and a diminishing number of candidates for ordination have added to the problem of providing the parishes with adequate staffing. Yet all who live within the parish can claim the service of the local church for Baptism, marriage and burial, and there are many other needs, physical, social, and spiritual, which the welfare state is unable to meet. The people of God in each parish have a responsibility as far as they are able, to show God's love in a ministry of care and compassion, willingly offered because they know God cares for them.

Such a ministry cannot be left to the ordained clergy alone. All who are called to belong to the people of God are also called to share in the ministry of the Church. By your Confirmation you are ordained into the priesthood of all believers.

> 'You are a chosen race, a royal priesthood, a dedicated nation, and a people claimed by God for his own, to proclaim the triumphs of him who has called you out of darkness into his marvellous light.'[81]

Peter wrote those words to lay men and women in the first century Church. Although some are called to a special priestly office of word and sacraments, all committed men and women have a priestly role. It is not a second class ministry. Sometimes it is said that the job of the laity is to support the clergy. It is the other way about. It is the laity who are in the front line of the Christian ministry. It is the task of the professional ministers, as Paul said, 'to equip God's people for work in his service'.[82]

Happily in recent years churches within the Anglican Communion have come to see the value of the laity sharing ministry with the clergy. Already they can take a significant share in the leadership of worship. But their ministry must be exercised in many other different ways. Visitors to the church can be welcomed, and awkward members of the congregation (almost every church has its quota of 'lame ducks') can be especially cared for and supported. Some lay people have gifts and experience which enable them to make a valuable contribution in helping in confirmation classes, preparing couples for marriage, counselling those facing marital breakdown supporting those with difficulties after bereavement, and visiting the sick and the lonely. In parishes where new housing areas are being established, or where there is much mobility of population, the local church can make a valuable impact through lay visiting or street warden schemes. The purpose of such visiting is, in the first instance, to make a friendly contact and to offer the kind of practical help and information newcomers usually need. Later a deeper relationship between the church and the new residents may be established.

There are wider needs of the secular community which the local church may be able to meet through the ministry of the laity. There are many who slip through the welfare safety net, and there are the socially disadvantaged who do not easily gain the sympathy of the public. In response to Christ's call to care, the local church must continue to keep its eyes alert for the unloved and the unlovely who are often unnoticed or deliberately ignored by those who are concerned to 'do good' to their neighbours. Families at risk, the single homeless, ex-prisoners, young people on the run from home, battered wives, drug addicts, homosexuals seeking a fair deal from 're-spectable' society, and the mentally disturbed, are among the many goups who should excite the active compassion of the followers of Jesus, who publicly took sides with those whom society at large was prepared to consign to the rubbish dump. Sometimes churches in an area (working, perhaps, through the local council of churches) can take the initiative in meeting these needs by setting up a 'half way house' for ex-psychiatric patients or a hostel for young people at risk. More often members of the local church can find opportunities for caring in collaboration with other voluntary organizations such as Gingerbread (for one parent families), Roots (for homeless men), Mind (for the mentally handicapped), the Samaritans, Shelter, and Women's and Children's Aid (for battered wives), organizations for ex-prisoners (such as NACRO) and much else. In some areas of the United Kingdom, Christians have come together to foster imaginative projects to bring help to the unemployed.

But can this be legitimately seen as part of the mission of the local church? Certainly, for not only must caring and compassion be seen to be the marks of those who claim the name of Christian (and if it is not seen the rest of their mission falls to the ground), but also those who live in daily communion with Jesus and pray for his Spirit, should be able to bring to the service of their fellow men particular qualities of patience, perseverance, and hope, believing that in every situation, however dark, there is a possibility of resurrection.

This is the ministry to which Baptism and Confirmation calls men and women in the world today. The opportunities are endless. The grace which God gives to fulfil it is boundless.

The wider Church

Today the Church of England is mother to a large world-wide family. If the parent is a little tired, her offspring are lively and growing rapidly. By your Confirmation you are admitted into this great family too. How did it come about? With the growth of the British Empire in the eighteenth and nineteenth centuries, chaplains and missionaries went overseas to unknown lands with the explorers, traders, adventurers, armies and those who had decided to emigrate from their homeland to seek their fortunes abroad. There is an epic quality to the stories of the old established missionary societies pioneering to bring the Gospel to areas not yet explored. The oldest missionary society, the Society for the Promotion of Christian Knowledge, came into being in 1698. Three years later the Society for the Propagation of the Gospel in Foreign Parts (its original title) was formed. Its name was changed to the United Society for the Propagation of the Gospel (USPG) when it later merged with the Universities Mission to Central Africa which had been founded in 1857 in response to David Livingstone's call. In 1799 the Church Missionary Society came into being as 'an association of persons united in obedience to the call of God to gather the people of all races into the Fellowship of Christ's Church'. Other societies have been formed more recently as new needs have had to be met. The Church of England has chosen to meet its responsibilities for world mission through these independant societies and almost every parish has links with one or other of them providing church members with the opportunity of praying, learning, and giving for the work of the Church overseas. As new churches were established in many parts of the world by Church of England missionaries, they initially came under the direction of the Archbishop of Canterbury or the Bishop of London. But the great distances involved made effective guidance from far away England increasingly difficult. The consecration of Samuel Seabury in Aberdeen in 1784 to be the first bishop of the Protestant Episcopal Church in the United States, in full communion with Canterbury, but not controlled by it, marked the beginning of the Anglican Communion as we now know it. Soon bishops in other parts of the world were consecrated to take charge of independent dioceses, linked with the mother Church in England but not under its direction. Today there are more than four hundred dioceses within the Anglican Communion, and several new ones are added each year. Churches within the Anglican family are to be found in Australia and New Zealand, Burma, South America, many parts of Africa and Asia (including China and Japan), in the United States and Canada, the South Pacific and the West Indies, and, nearer home, the Church in Wales, the Episcopal Church of Scotland, and the Church of Ireland. This is no longer a communion of churches for white men or English speakers only. In Africa blacks are in the majority in Anglican churches, and their number grows rapidly. The Bible and Prayer Book are printed in many different languages. Today the total number of Anglicans in the world is in excess of sixty-five million. All these churches are independent. All owe their origin to the missionary work of the Church of England, or, more recently, other Anglican churches. All are in communion with the see of Canterbury, recognizing in the Archbishop their common focus of unity. All have based their beliefs, worship and ministry on the Book of Common Prayer, though each national church is free to make what alterations it thinks necessary. This is why some Anglican provinces ordain women to the priesthood and others do not.

If you travel within the Anglican family you will notice both similarities and differences in the various orders of worship in use. Your own local parish church is part of this world-wide fellowship. By Baptism and Confirmation you become part of it too. Never lose sight of this dimension of your faith. As a committed Christian you must be a true internationalist.

The Anglican Communion is not one of the largest bodies in Christendom, but it has a special contribution to bring to the wider Christian Church. The combination of 'high' and 'low' elements, which have been such a feature in the story of the development of the Church of England, gives Anglicans the opportunity of understanding something of both Catholic and Protestant tradition, thought and practice, and so acting as a kind of bridge. In those steps towards the unity of churches separated from one another, which are called the ecumenical movement, Anglicans have been able to play a significant part. Most of the Churches within the Anglican family have been engaged in serious conversation with Methodists, Presbyterians, Lutherans, Baptists and others to see how divisions can be healed in their own countries. In some places Anglicans have been ready to enter into newly formed united Churches. Anglicans in many parts of the world, not least in the new nations of Africa and Asia, are among the three hundred churches from a hundred countries which form the World Council of Churches. Each country has its own national ecumenical council, such as the British Council of Churches in which successive Archbishops of Canterbury have played a leading part. So Anglicans can claim to have made an important contribution to this essential work of unity for the sake of mission and witness. Much remains to be done.

As a member of your local parish church you will find your greatest opportunity for involvement in the unity movement through the work of your own local council of churches or ecumenical group in your neighbourhood. There are nearly 700 councils of churches in the British Isles. They vary considerably in their effectiveness. Some have ambitious programmes of joint worship, study, witness, and social action. Others are content with occasional meetings and united services, often poorly attended because the participating churches fail to give the support and publicity they deserve. If you believe (as you should) that the movement towards the unity of our divided Churches is an essential part of our commitment to mission, you will do all you can to take your share in whatever the Christians of your neighbourhood are able to plan together.

You will quickly discover that the things we have in common are far greater (and more important) than the things that still divide us. Anglicans have a special opportunity of entering into a positive relationship with Roman Catholics not only because of the 'thaw' since the second Vatican Council and the visit of Pope John Paul II to Britain (and Canterbury Cathedral) in 1982, but also because of the significant findings of the report of the Anglican-Roman Catholic International Commission

(ARCIC). If you want to find out how much Anglicans and Roman Catholics agree (and disagree) about the Eucharist, the Ministry, and the authority of the Church (including the role of the Papacy), this report is well worth studying, and discussing with your Roman Catholic neighbours.[83]

The best known ecumenical activity in Britain today is Christian Aid. This is a massive piece of united action by British Churches of all denominations to provide in the name of Christ for the poor, the oppressed, the persecuted, the hungry, the homeless, the illiterate in our unjust and unequal world. The money raised for Christian Aid by the churches together in this country is applied in the areas of need by the churches working together overseas. Givers and receivers become partners in mission by this shared action. Christian Aid is not simply a money raising agency. It is a powerful instrument with which Christian men and women can learn about the needs of mankind and respond not only by their generosity, but also by their informed concern and their prayers. This ecumenical dimension to our Christian life is not to be seen as an optional extra which we might possibly care to consider when we have 'done our own thing' in our own church. You are not baptized and confirmed solely into the Anglican Communion. You are made a part of the world-wide Church of Jesus Christ. An active ecumenical concern, beginning in your own neighbourhood, is the best way of discovering this fact for yourself.

Christian character

Confirmation is not a passing out parade or a ceremony to mark the end of an examination course which, when completed, may be soon forgotten. It is the start of adult Christian life, the planting of good seed in well prepared soil, hopefully soon to grow quickly into flower. After the laying on of hands the bishop invites all present to join in a prayer asking that those who have been confirmed may continue faithful to the promise they have made and may 'daily increase in the Holy Spirit'. The seed has been planted. Now the prayer is offered that it may grow well.

By what signs will you be able to tell that this prayer is being answered? What are the marks of a true Christian character? A valuable guide by which you will be able to discern the growth of the Spirit within yourself can be found in the list of the fruits of the Spirit which Paul gave to the Galatians. They are, he told them, love, joy, peace, patience, kindness, goodness, fidelity, gentleness, and self control. There is no finer check list against which to measure the Christian character.[84]

Love is the greatest of all Christian virtues because more than any other this is the word we use to speak about the nature of God himself. The Bible dares to say that God is not only lovely and loving but that he is himself love. The Christian understanding of love goes beyond the love of a man and woman for each other, or the love you may have of friends, music, sport or country. Love is that deepest concern that someone can have for another's total well-being, whether he likes the other person or not. Paul's great poem in praise of love has become the classic description of this greatest of all qualities.[85] The origin and source of love is in God himself. When Jesus taught that a man should love his enemies as well as his friends, he said that 'your heavenly Father makes the sun rise on good and bad alike, and sends his rain on the honest and the dishonest'.[86] The heart of Christian preaching is that Christ did not wait for us to repent and turn over a new leaf before showing his love for us. He died for us while we were yet sinners. This is not the way the world thinks. Most love songs are selfish. 'I will love you for what I expect to get in return.' Instead of loving their enemies most people think in terms of revenge. Because it goes against the tide of popular action, Christ's kind of loving is costly. To the outsider it looks weak. The Christian knows that love is the strongest power on earth, and points to his Lord crucified upon a cross to prove it.

Joy. The chief end of man, says the older Shorter Catechism, is to glorify God and to enjoy him forever. But joy in the vocabulary of the Christian goes much deeper than the 'feverish thirst for pleasure' of which a hymn speaks, and which often brings no joy at all. For many the search for joy is an attempt to escape from the harsh realities of life and to find an occasional relief from the day to day trials of human existence. There is a place for this kind of temporary respite. But it is nothing to do with true joy which comes not from running away from life, but by coming closer to God. 'You have not seen Jesus, yet you love him; and trusting in him now without seeing him, are transported with a joy too great for words.'[87] Joy is the antidote to that spirit of cynicism and disillusionment which can be soul destroying. Its focus is not on our failures but on God's powerful love. True joy is not a question of whistling in the dark to keep your spirits up. Its springs are deep in the experience of God himself, and its waters can refresh every part of life. Nor does it offer merely a temporary deliverance. Jesus promised that no man can rob us of his joy.[88]

Peace. The Hebrew word *Shalom* has come into popular use lately. It is a valuable word, and has no precise equivalent in English. It conveys the sense of wholeness, well-being and harmony. Its opposite is the feeling of being 'at sixes and sevens' with oneself and at odds with the world. Peace is God's gift both to the individual and to the life of the community. We cannot search for it relying solely on our own resources. Peace, like love and joy comes from God, and we long for it because we were created by him. As Augustine of Hippo said 'Thou hast created us for thyself, and our hearts cannot be quieted until they find their rest in thee'. Jesus promised his disciples peace and after his resurrection he greeted them with a sign of peace. Thus *shalom* became a Christian greeting and in many Anglican churches it now has a central place in the Eucharist. Jesus also taught that this inner peace would come from a detachment from the temporal things of life. You will find peace by refusing to allow concern for money, prestige 'getting on' and other pre-occupations of success to become your dominant obsession. If you cultivate an inner peace you are unlikely to find yourself at the mercy of changing circumstances. And if you have peace within yourself, you will bring an atmosphere of inner quiet, serenity, *shalom* to those about you.

Patience. Here is a difficult quality to achieve in a restless world. We shall only understand it by contemplating the patience of God. 'Thou, Lord, art God, compassionate and gracious, forbearing, ever constant and true.' [89] Jesus is shown in the Gospels as patient with his disciples even when they must have tried him sorely. In his humiliation and crucifixion he revealed an unbelievable patience in the face of terrible injustice. Bible writers speak continually of God's patience as an example we are meant to follow. Paul asked the Christians in Rome 'Do you think lightly of his wealth of kindness, of tolerance, and of patience, without recognizing that

God's kindness is meant to lead you to a change of heart?'[90] How quickly we get impatient with other people, and even with ourselves. The only impatience we should show is for the coming of God's kingdom and for peace, justice and well-being for all people everywhere.

Kindness follows naturally from what has gone before. 'Love is very patient, very kind.' Kindness is that quality of loving which opens our eyes to the needs of other people, and then compels us to do something practical about it. In one of his most powerful parables Jesus taught that acts of practical kindness to the hungry, the thirsty, the stranger, the naked, the sick and the imprisoned are acts of kindness to God himself.[91] Kindness must never remain a matter of feeling. It must always lead from feeling to action. It is so easy for the more emotional of us to weep over the disasters reported in the newspapers or which overtake our favourite soap opera characters on television. But there is danger in having our feelings of pity stimulated when we are not in a position to do something practical in response. The Scouts and Guides are on the right track with their daily good turn. Kindness which does not lead to some sort of practical action is not kindness at all.

Goodness. This is a word which frightens us. Nobody wants to be thought a 'goody-goody'. In his readings from St John's Gospel William Temple translated the 'good shepherd' as 'the shepherd, the beautiful one'. He commented:

> 'It is important that the word for good here is one that represents, not the moral rectitude of goodness, nor its authority, but its attractiveness. We must not forget that our vocation is so to practise virtue that men are won by it; it is possible to be morally upright repulsively.'[92]

One of the Psalms talks of the 'beauty of holiness'. It is so easy for goodness to seem rather ugly. Jesus attracted men and women to him by the sheer beauty of his personality and character. You are called, as a follower of Jesus, to shed your light among your fellows so that 'when they see the good you do, they may give praise to your Father in heaven'.[93]

Fidelity. Trustworthiness is an essential feature of the disciple of Christ who knows that he can put his trust in God who trusts him. Jesus told a number of stories about a king or a boss who went away to a far country trusting his people to get on with the job in his absence.[94] We are given by God an astonishing degree of freedom to live our lives as we think best. He is not for ever fussing to see how we are doing. He trusts us to be faithful to him, and to stay the course. As you commit yourself in your Confirmation, you can be certain that God is trusting you to be faithful in prayer, worship, belief and service. You can trust him to keep his part of the bargain. The rest is up to you.

Gentleness. It is said that the people of the ancient world refused to see gentleness as a virtue. Perhaps it is equally true today. The cult figures in the television serials, the cowboys, detectives, space astronauts and the denizens of Dallas all present an image of toughness. 'Gentle Jesus meek and mild' does not seem to be an appropriate picture to put before a child growing up in an age of soap operas and science fiction. Yet Jesus, who lived as we do in a violent world, was not ashamed to speak of himself as gentle. He urged his followers to 'bend your necks to my yoke, and learn from me, for I am gentle and humble-hearted; and your souls will find relief'.[95] Those of a gentle spirit will be blessed, he said in the beatitudes, with the promise that they will gain the earth. Paul, when he was dealing with some tough situations in the Corinthian church wrote 'I appeal to you by the gentleness and magnanimity of Christ.'[96] It is part of human experience that forceful opposition can sometimes be overcome by gentleness when a tough stand will only aggravate the situation. Gentleness is a sign of strength, not weakness. You must not see it as a negative quality, for it was one of the outstanding characteristics of Jesus Christ himself.

Self control. Paul introduced his list of the fruits of the Spirit by describing their opposites which he called 'the behaviour which belongs to the lower nature'. These include fornication, impurity, indecency, quarrels, contentious temper, rage, dissension, drinking bouts and orgies.[97] Far from being signs of human freedom, these things indicate that man no longer has control over himself. He has become a slave to sin, and is in need of liberation. Freedom returns when self-discipline is recovered. Paul likens this discipline to the training an athlete must undergo if he is to succeed. 'I am like a boxer who does not beat the air: I bruise my body and make it know its master'.[98] This discipline is not only necessary for avoiding the sins of the body such as greed and lust, but also those failures of personality which threaten all of us, envy, pride, impatience, covetousness, and laziness. These dangers to our Christian living require constant vigilance and a continual reappraisal of the acts of self denial which we know are essential for our spiritual health.

Christian rule

At your Confirmation your fellow Christians who will be your witnesses will pray that you will daily increase in the

Holy Spirit more and more. That prayer cannot be answered without your active co-operation. You must be determined from this point onwards to grow continually in love and obedience to God, and to be faithful disciples. This will only happen if:

(a) you grow in your understanding of the meaning and relevance of the Bible and of the faith you have professed;

(b) you resolve to make the practice of prayer a regular feature of your life;

(c) you join regularly with your fellow Christians in worship, and especially in receiving the sacrament of the Holy Communion each Sunday unless you are reasonably prevented from doing so;

(d) you give generously of your time, your money and your talents for the furthering of the work and witness of the church of Jesus Christ in your locality;

(e) you endeavour increasingly to show the Spirit of Christ in every part of your life — in your marriage and family life, in your personal relationships, in your daily work, in your concern for those in need, and in your social and political commitment as a citizen of your country and of the world;

(f) you make regular acts of self examination and assessment to check up on your progress as a Christian pilgrim, to ask forgiveness when you have followed false trails, and to make resolutions for future advancement in your spiritual life.

Bible Reading. If you have not already done so, equip yourself with a good modern translation of the Bible. Some people prefer the Authorized Version because of the beauty of its language. But modern translations generally take us closer to what the authors originally wrote because there have been great advances in biblical scholarship in recent years. The new versions are usually easier to understand. Having equipped yourself with a Bible, be sure you use it. If in time your Bible begins to look rather shabby, with underlinings and notes scribbled in the margins, that is a good sign. The Bible is not meant to be kept in brand new condition behind the glass doors of a bookcase.

Most people are helped in their Bible reading if they use one or other of the various series of daily notes which are easily available.

Many people derive additional benefit from doing their Bible study in small groups, often meeting in one another's houses. It is worth while finding out whether such a group meets in your parish or neighbourhood. You could even take the initiative of starting one if necessary. Such groups are often ecumenical. They can begin by using one of the sets of Bible reading notes, or by reading together one of the Gospels. You would also be wise to back up your Bible study with wider reading about the Christian faith. There are a large number of inexpensive paperbacks on religious subjects available, and you may feel you would like to tackle a few of the bigger hardbacks which are likely to be more demanding. Unfortunately most general booksellers have a very poor stock (if any) of books about religion, but in the larger towns there are usually bookstores specializing in Christian literature, and an afternoon spent browsing in one of these is time well spent. Some churches today have small lending libraries or bookstalls. If there is not one in your church you might be able to persuade someone (yourself?) to get one going.

Prayer and Worship. You need at least the minimum equipment to help you in your devotional life. This includes a prayer book (the ASB, BCP or its equivalent in other parts of the Anglican Communion), a few books of prayers and a notebook (preferably loose-leaf), for your own prayer calendar. Having equipped yourself, you need to make a plan of action for your prayer life, stick firmly to it, and review it from time to time. Although there will be moments of great joy and profound sorrow when you will be driven to your knees, it is not good normally to rely on saying your prayers only when you feel like it. You will soon find that you like it less and less. You have to make rules for yourself, and be prepared to keep them. But be sure to plan your prayer scheme in a way that is practically possible for you, which makes neither too great nor too few demands, and which will fit into your own particular style of life. No two people are quite the same, and you have to find your own level. Traditionally the time for prayer is when you go to bed at night and get up in the morning. For some this is the most practical way of doing it. For others it is impossible. Some find it convenient to put aside time during the day for prayer and Bible study. Others form the habit of going into a nearby church for their daily devotions. Initially you will certainly want help and advice on the best plan for yourself. Your parish clergy are there to help you on matters of this sort.

Prayer is like a symphony or a play, it must proceed through a number of movements or acts, each logically following on what has gone before. It should begin with a clear focus on God, with expressions of praise and joy. The Bible can get you off to a good start, for it helps you to know that God is at work, and to hear what he wants to say to you. Prayer should be as much (perhaps more) about listening to God as it is about talking to him. Praise leads naturally to thanksgiving, not only for the benefits which we have received but in gratitude that we can know God through Jesus Christ, and the confidence that he knows us and promises to give us his Spirit to be our companion in our daily lives. Having brought ourselves consciously into the presence of God, we recognize our failure to respond to his love. So we make an act of penitence for the many ways in which we have failed to do that. It is when we have cleared our consciences, confident in God's power to forgive us, that we are in a fit state to bring to him our own needs and those of our friends. This is where the loose-leaf book can come into use. We cannot pray for everybody every day, though some people will have a more frequent claim upon our prayers than others. We can make a prayer calendar weekly or monthly, so that we can offer regular intercessions not only for our families, friends, neighbours, colleagues at work and the local church, but also include the wider needs of our country and our world. Prayer should always lead to some kind of action. Because we have prayed we may be moved to telephone someone, write a long delayed letter, pay a much overdue bill, visit someone who is ill or lonely, patch up a quarrel, or take positive steps to put right those things in ourselves which we know have gone wrong.

This pattern of prayer can be well used following the reading of a Bible passage. Having read the chosen section, your prayers can flow easily from it. What do these words say to me:

about the glory of God,
about the things I should thank God for,
about the things for which I must ask forgiveness,
about the prayers I must offer for others as well as
    myself,
about the practical resolutions I must make?
Because all prayer (even if done in the privacy of our

108

own room) is offered in the context of the whole Church, some Anglicans like to base their prayers on the set pattern of daily worship set out in the Prayer book, using the Bible readings in the official lectionary of the Church. The short form of Morning and Evening Prayer in the ASB is well suited for private devotion as well as for public worship. The ASB also contains a good selection of collects and other prayers which can be used at home.

The chief expression of our membership of the world-wide Church of Jesus Christ is in our regular attendance at the Eucharist. The meaning of this central act of Christian worship has been discussed in a previous section. Enough to say here that you should never go to this great sacrament casually or unprepared. In particular you should think out in advance what particular praises, thanksgivings, penitence, intercessions, petitions and resolutions you want to bring with you to offer to God as the service proceeds. A general act of thanksgiving, confession and prayer can mean so much more to you if you are able to recollect specific items relevant to yourself as each new stage of the service is reached. And do not forget to say 'Thank you' when the service is over.

You must not expect that your prayers, either in your own home or with your fellow Christians in church will always provide you with a feeling of excitement and assurance. There are times when prayer becomes dull, and you begin to wonder whether anyone is there. These are the moment when it is hardest to concentrate, and when perseverance is most worthwhile. Bishop Michael Ramsey has words of encouragement for you.

> 'There are times when prayer vibrates with joy and eagerness, and there are times when the brain seems stupider than ever, the imagination wanders far

away, and the feelings are cold and the will very weak. At such a time it may be the best course simply to repeat acts of wanting God, of wanting to pray, of wanting to love, of wanting to have faith, not shrinking from the repetition of the phrases. To pray thus is to expose one's own weakness in God's presence and to ask him to use our little fragments of wanting and loving beyond what we ask or have. If the enthusiasm of a full heart brings us near to God, no less near to him is the prayer of a frail sincere wanting. It may open the soul to a new pouring in of love of God.'

Growth. A flower bed not only needs constant doses of fertilizer to refresh the soil, it needs constant continual weeding so that the new growth is not choked. The Christian who wishes to increase daily in the Holy Spirit not only needs the refreshment and encouragement which comes from worship. He also needs to weed out all the bad things which hinder his growth in the life of the Spirit. You must avoid extremes. You should not forever be taking your spiritual temperature, for that can develop into a morbid introspection. Nor should you pretend that all is well with you, for that leads to a self congratulatory complacency. You should neither suppress your feelings of guilt, nor wallow in them. Learn to be healthily self-critical. The list of the fruits of the Spirit in the letter to the Galatians provides one means of self testing. The ten commandments and the beatitudes will enable you to see how you stand before God. If you feel worried with a sense of failure in your faith or worship or daily life, and feel that spiritually you are standing still rather than going forward, your parish priest may be able to help you. It is a tradition in the Anglican Communion to make available, for those who wish, the sacrament of confession and absolution before the priest. This provision dates from the first Church of England Prayer Book which, in an exhortation in the Communion service, urged anyone unable to quieten his conscience before coming to the sacrament, and who feels the need for assurance and advice, to come to the priest to 'open his grief, that by the ministry of God's Holy Word he may receive the benefit of absolution, together with ghostly (spiritual) counsel and advice to the quieting of his conscience'. It is often thought that 'going to confession' is a 'high' church thing to do, and it is in Anglo-Catholic churches that it is more obviously available. But it is part of the Anglican tradition that although none must be compelled to confess before a priest, it should be on hand for any who believe they would benefit from this confidential ministry. Some people find it particularly helpful to make their confession before some great occasion such as Confirmation or marriage, or in preparation for a major festival of the Church. If you feel that this would be useful to your own spiritual growth, you should discuss it carefully with a priest skilled in this ministry (not necessarily your own minister) before making a final decision about it.

Other opportunities for exercise in growth can be found in the many retreats and conferences now available for lay people. Although silent retreats are considered by some to be rather old fashioned, many still find them of great value. Just to get away to some pleasant place and be quiet for a while in an atmosphere of prayer is a rare refreshment in this noisy and busy world. If you cannot bear the thought of a week of silence, most retreat houses organize week-end retreats and especially welcome those who are making a retreat for the first time. Most dioceses have retreat houses from which a programme of arrangements can be had.

To commit yourself to Christ as a member of his Church, and to share in his mission to the world of your time is a great adventure. It is a pilgrimage into the unknown future, for we never know what it is that God has in store for us. Karl Rahner, the German Roman Catholic theologian was fond of emphasizing this point. 'We must recognize soberly', he once told the synod of Catholic bishops in his own country, 'that no planning of the Church's future in the next decade can relieve us of the necessity of going forward into the future that cannot be planned, of risk, of danger, and of hope in the incalculable grace of God.' To belong to the Church is to share in that pilgrimage. We do not know where the journey will lead. But we do know who is leading us, and we have in the life of prayer, Bible study and sacrament the rations we need for our journey. As travelling companions we have an innumerable company of fellow Christians. For our part, we must ask for grace to persevere, praying with Sir Francis Drake, a great adventurer in the reign of Elizabeth I:

O Lord God, when thou givest to thy servant to endeavour any great matter, grant us able to know that it is not the beginning, but the continuing of the same until the end, until it be thoroughly finished, which yieldeth the true glory. Amen.

FOR FURTHER THOUGHT AND DISCUSSION ON BEING AN ANGLICAN

Here is a check-list of twelve questions.

1. Do you know the history of your local parish church?

2. Do you know who are the members of your parochial church council?
3. Are you on the electoral or membership roll of your church?
4. Do you receive your parish magazine (if there is one) and other literature from your local church?
5. Do you know what activities and organizations your church provides?
6. Do you know what plans your church makes for mission and social outreach?
7. Does your church have a stewardship or regular giving scheme? Are you involved in it?
8. Do you make an effort to get to know your fellow worshippers? How?
9. Have you ever visited your diocesan cathedral to see what happens there?
10. What opportunities does your local church give you for learning about the world-wide Anglican Communion, and sharing in its work by your gifts and prayers?
11. What opportunities have you of meeting, worshipping and working with members of other denominations?
12. What particularly attracts you to the Anglican Church?

For your prayers.

Lord our God, giver of all grace, have mercy on your Church throughout the world.
   Renew its life;
   restore its unity;
   sanctify its worship;
   empower its witness;
   and make it a fit instrument for the furtherance of

Christ's kingdom among men, to the glory of his great name.

(*Frank Colquhoun*)

APPENDIX A

REFERENCES

Chapter 1   Initiation
1. Philippians 3. 12-14
2. Romans 6. 1-4
3. Acts 8. 14-17 and Acts 19. 1-7

Chapter 2   Discipleship
4. These events are described with interesting variations in Matthew 16.13-17.20, Mark 8. 27-9.29, and Luke 9. 18-43
5. 2 Peter 1. 16-17. Most scholars believe that this letter was not written by Peter himself, but these verses show the importance the early Church attached to the story of the transfiguration of Christ.
6. Luke 9.39
7. 1 Peter 3.15

Chapter 3   Belief
8. Romans 8. 22-23
9. Exodus 33.11
10. Psalm 103.13
11. Hosea 11. 1-2
12. Isaiah 54.5
13. 1 Corinthians 1.18-24
14. 1 Thessalonians 4.14
15. 1 Corinthians 15. 1-7
16. Acts 2. 23-24
17. Romans 3. 25-26 (Good News Bible)
18. 2 Corinthians 5.21 (Good News Bible)

19. *see* Romans 8. 31-39
20. John 17.3
21. For Paul's teaching on the resurrection of the body *see* 1 Corinthians 15. 35-57
22. *see* Eberhard Bethge's foreword to his edition of *Letters and Papers from Prison* by Dietrich Bonhoeffer (SCM Press)
23. Luke 1.36 (Good News Bible)
24. Mark 1.10 (Good News Bible)
25. Luke 4. 14-18
26. Matthew 12. 31-32
27. *see* John 14-16
28. John 7.39
29. John 20. 19-23
30. Acts 2. 1-21
31. Genesis 11. 1-9
32. Galatians 5. 22-23 (Good News Bible)
33. Matthew 28.19
34. Genesis 2.18

Chapter 4   Worship
35. Genesis 3.9
36. Psalm 139. 1-2 (ASB)
37. Basil Hume, *To be a Pilgrim* (SPCK)
38. Luke 5.16
39. Mark 6.31
40. Luke 6.12
41. Luke 22.42
42. Matthew 6.9-13

43. Galatians 4.6-7
44. Psalm 20.7
45. Philippians 2. 9-l0
46. 1 Thessalonians 5.16
47. Jude 24
48. Luke 4.18-21
49. Luke 7. 18-23
50. Luke 21. 8-11
51. Luke 17. 21
52. It is worth reading carefully the parables about the kingdom of God which you will find in Matthew 13. 1-52.
53. John 4.34
54. Hebrews 7.25
55. William Cowper (1731-1800) in the hymn 'God moves in a mysterious way'.
56. Matthew 6. 31-34
57. Luke 11. 5-13
58. Luke 18. 1-8
59. Michael Ramsey, *Be Still and Know* (Fount)
60. Philippians 1.19
61. Romans 3.23
62. 1 John 1.8
63. Romans 5.8
64. Hans Küng, *On being a Christian* (Fount)
65. Matthew 18. 23-35
66. James 1.13
67. Luke 22. 31-32
68. Corinthians 12.7-10
69. Hebrews 4.15
70. 1 Corinthians 10.13

Chapter 5   Service
71. James 1.27 and 2.17
72. John 13. 1-17
73. Acts 8.4
74. Matthew 5. 13-16

Chapter 6   Being an Anglican
75. Exodus 6.7
76. John 15. 1-10
77. 1 Corinthians 12. 1-12
78. Peter 2.10
79. Acts 2.42
80. Corinthians 1. 26-30
81. 1 Peter 2.9
82. Ephesians 4.12
83. *Anglican-Roman Catholic International Commission. The Final Report* (CTS, SPCK)
84. Galatians 5. 22-25
85. 1 Corinthians 13
86. Matthew 5.45
87. 1 Peter 1.8
88. John 16.22
89. Psalm 86.15
90. Romans 2.4
91. Matthew 25. 31-46
92. William Temple, *Readings in St John's Gospel* (Macmillan)
93. Matthew 5.16
94. for example, Matthew 25. 14-30
95. Matthew 11. 28-30
96. 2 Corinthians 10.1
97. Galatians 5.19
98. 1 Corinthians 9. 24-27

APPENDIX B

For further reading

About the Bible

Modern Bible translations:
  New English Bible (Oxford and Cambridge University Presses)
  The New Jerusalem Bible (Darton, Longman & Todd)
  The Good News Bible (Collins)
  New International Bible (Hodder & Stoughton)
  Revised Standard Version (The Bible Societies/Collins)

If you want more information about daily Bible reading notes, write to:
  The Bible Reading Fellowship, St Michael's House, 2 Elizabeth Street, London SW1W 9RQ;
  The Scripture Union, 130 City Road, London EC1V 2NJ.

If you want to choose a book of the Bible to study day by day, you will find almost every book of the Bible available in *The Daily Study Bible*, William Barclay (St Andrew's Press, Edinburgh).
Other recommended commentaries to help you in more detailed study of the Bible are:
  Torch Bible Commentaries (SCM Press)
  Cambridge Bible Commentaries on the New English Bible (Cambridge University Press)

To help you in the background to your Bible study:
  Open the Book, Edward Patey (Mowbray)
  What is the Bible? Neville B. Cryer (Mowbray's Enquirer's Library)
  Can we trust the Old Testament? William Neil (Mowbray)
  Can we trust the New Testament? J.A.T. Robinson (Mowbray)

About belief

Being a Christian, Richard Harries (Mowbray)
All in Good Faith, Edward H. Patey (Mowbray)
What Anglicans Believe, David L. Edwards (Mowbray)
A Pocket Guide to Christian Belief, Jean Smith (Mowbray)
and in Mowbray's Enquirer's Library:
Learning about Jesus, Arthur Moore
Learning about the Holy Spirit, G.C.B. Davies
Learning about the Resurrection, G.C.B. Davies

If you are prepared to read a much larger book demanding careful thought and attention, try *On Being a Christian*, Hans Küng (Fount)

About prayer

Be Still and Know, Michael Ramsey (Fount)
Turning to Prayer, Richard Harries (Mowbray)
The Practice of Prayer, George Appleton (Mowbray)
Praying Round the Clock, Richard Harries (Mowbray)
Prayer and Contemplation, Mark Gibbard (Mowbray)
Prayer for Beginners, John Ryeland (Mowbray)
A Communicant's Manual, William Purcell (Mowbray)
*The Quiet Heart, Prayers and meditations for each day of the
    year,* George Appleton (Fount)
To be a Pilgrim, Basil Hume (SPCK)
and in Mowbray's Enquirer's Library:
Learning about Private Prayer, Desmond Tillyer
Learning to Pray, Michael Turnbull
Learning about Retreats, Sister Joanna Baldwin

About Your Local Church

Open the doors. The mission of the local church. Edward
    Patey (Mowbray)
Learning about the PCC, Anthony Boult (Mowbray's En-
    quirer's Library)
An ABC for the PCC, John Pitchford (Mowbray)

118

About the Anglican Communion

A Pocket Guide to the Anglican Church, Ronald H. Lloyd (Mowbray)

Learning about the Church of England, Michael Smith (Mowbray's Enquirer's Library)

Anglicanism, Stephen Neill (Mowbray)

The Anglican Church Today and Tomorrow, Michael Marshall (Mowbray)

About the Christian Life

Christian Life Style, Edward Patey (Mowbray)

Christian Marriage, Helen Lee (Mowbray)

I give you this ring, Edward Patey (Mowbray)

and in Mowbray's Enquirer's Library:

Christianity and Sex, Edward Patey

Learning about Christian Giving, Roger V. Chadwick

Stewardship and Sharing, Phyllis Carter

Alcoholism, Terry Drummond

Bereavement, William Purcell

Divorce, Wendy Green

Learning about Christian Health and Healing, Norman Autton

Making Use of Illness, Norman Autton

Learning to cope with Depression, D.R. Copestake

Learning to cope with Loneliness, Anne Arnott

Suffering and the Christian Response, Mary Endersbee